50 Elevated Campfire Cooking Recipes for Home

By: Kelly Johnson

Table of Contents

- Grilled Skirt Steak with Chimichurri Sauce
- Campfire Dutch Oven Lasagna
- Spicy Shrimp and Sausage Skewers
- Cedar Plank Salmon with Maple Glaze
- Campfire Pizza with Fresh Mozzarella and Basil
- Stuffed Bell Peppers with Ground Turkey and Quinoa
- Foil Packet Cajun Chicken and Vegetables
- Grilled Veggie Quesadillas with Avocado Cream
- Campfire Jambalaya with Andouille Sausage and Shrimp
- Grilled Portobello Mushrooms Stuffed with Goat Cheese and Spinach
- Campfire Beef and Bean Chili
- Lemon Herb Chicken Skewers with Greek Yogurt Sauce
- Foil Packet Garlic Butter Shrimp
- Grilled Halibut Tacos with Mango Salsa
- Campfire Paella with Chorizo and Seafood
- BBQ Pulled Pork Stuffed Sweet Potatoes
- Grilled Zucchini Ribbons with Pesto
- Foil Packet Lemon Garlic Chicken with Asparagus
- Campfire Ratatouille with Fresh Herbs
- Grilled Swordfish Steaks with Tomato Basil Relish
- Sweet and Spicy Korean BBQ Chicken Skewers
- Campfire Beef Stroganoff with Mushrooms
- Foil Packet Coconut-Lime Shrimp
- Grilled Eggplant Parmesan Stacks
- Campfire Cornbread Stuffed with Jalapenos and Cheddar
- Grilled Mahi Mahi Tacos with Pineapple Salsa
- Foil Packet Teriyaki Salmon and Veggies
- Campfire Risotto with Wild Mushrooms and Parmesan
- Grilled Thai Beef Salad with Peanut Dressing
- Campfire Veggie Stir-Fry with Tofu
- Foil Packet Lemon Dill Salmon with Green Beans
- Grilled Moroccan Lamb Kebabs with Yogurt Sauce
- Campfire Ratatouille Stuffed Peppers
- Grilled Octopus with Chimichurri Sauce
- Foil Packet BBQ Chicken and Potatoes

- Campfire Eggplant Involtini with Ricotta and Marinara
- Grilled Shrimp and Pineapple Skewers with Coconut Rice
- Campfire BBQ Brisket with Homemade BBQ Sauce
- Foil Packet Mediterranean Salmon with Olives and Tomatoes
- Grilled Chicken Shawarma Wraps with Tahini Sauce
- Campfire Stuffed Acorn Squash with Quinoa and Cranberries
- Grilled Scallops with Citrus-Herb Butter
- Foil Packet Garlic Herb Steak and Potatoes
- Campfire Ratatouille Flatbread Pizza
- Grilled Tuna Nicoise Salad with Dijon Vinaigrette
- Campfire Stuffed Portobello Mushrooms with Sun-Dried Tomatoes and Feta
- Grilled Lamb Chops with Mint Chimichurri Sauce
- Foil Packet Lemon Garlic Shrimp and Asparagus
- Campfire Cornish Hens with Herb Butter
- Grilled Vegetable Platter with Balsamic Glaze

Grilled Skirt Steak with Chimichurri Sauce

Ingredients:

For the Skirt Steak:

- 2 lbs skirt steak
- 2 tablespoons olive oil
- Salt and pepper to taste

For the Chimichurri Sauce:

- 1 cup fresh parsley, finely chopped
- 1/4 cup fresh cilantro, finely chopped
- 4 cloves garlic, minced
- 1 shallot, finely chopped
- 1/4 cup red wine vinegar
- 1/2 cup extra virgin olive oil
- 1 teaspoon dried oregano
- 1/2 teaspoon red pepper flakes (adjust to taste)
- Salt and pepper to taste

Instructions:

1. Start by preparing the chimichurri sauce. In a bowl, combine the finely chopped parsley, cilantro, minced garlic, chopped shallot, red wine vinegar, extra virgin olive oil, dried oregano, red pepper flakes, salt, and pepper. Stir well to combine. Set aside to let the flavors meld while you prepare the steak.
2. Preheat your grill to high heat.
3. Drizzle the skirt steak with olive oil and season generously with salt and pepper on both sides.
4. Place the seasoned skirt steak on the preheated grill. Cook for about 3-4 minutes per side for medium-rare, or adjust cooking time to your desired level of doneness.
5. Once the steak is cooked to your liking, remove it from the grill and let it rest for a few minutes to allow the juices to redistribute.
6. Slice the skirt steak against the grain into thin strips.

7. Serve the grilled skirt steak with chimichurri sauce drizzled over the top or on the side for dipping.
8. Enjoy your Grilled Skirt Steak with Chimichurri Sauce with your favorite sides, such as roasted vegetables, grilled potatoes, or a fresh salad.

This dish is bursting with flavor and is sure to impress your friends and family at your next outdoor gathering!

Campfire Dutch Oven Lasagna

Ingredients:

- 1 lb ground beef or Italian sausage
- 1 onion, chopped
- 3 cloves garlic, minced
- 1 can (28 oz) crushed tomatoes
- 1 can (15 oz) tomato sauce
- 1 can (6 oz) tomato paste
- 2 teaspoons dried basil
- 1 teaspoon dried oregano
- Salt and pepper to taste
- 9 lasagna noodles, uncooked
- 2 cups shredded mozzarella cheese
- 1 cup ricotta cheese
- 1/4 cup grated Parmesan cheese
- Fresh basil leaves for garnish (optional)

Instructions:

1. Prepare your campfire by setting up a stable area for your Dutch oven to sit securely over hot coals.
2. In a Dutch oven, cook the ground beef or Italian sausage over medium heat until browned, breaking it up into crumbles as it cooks.
3. Add the chopped onion and minced garlic to the Dutch oven and cook until the onion is softened, about 3-4 minutes.
4. Stir in the crushed tomatoes, tomato sauce, tomato paste, dried basil, dried oregano, salt, and pepper. Bring the sauce to a simmer and let it cook for about 10-15 minutes, stirring occasionally to prevent sticking.
5. Once the sauce is ready, remove the Dutch oven from the heat. Arrange a layer of lasagna noodles over the sauce, breaking them if necessary to fit.
6. Spread half of the ricotta cheese evenly over the noodles, followed by a layer of shredded mozzarella cheese.
7. Repeat the layers with half of the remaining sauce, the remaining lasagna noodles, the remaining ricotta cheese, and another layer of shredded mozzarella cheese.
8. Top the lasagna with the remaining sauce and sprinkle the grated Parmesan cheese over the top.

9. Cover the Dutch oven with its lid and place it over hot coals from your campfire. Cook for about 30-40 minutes, or until the lasagna noodles are tender and the cheese is melted and bubbly.
10. Once the lasagna is cooked, carefully remove the Dutch oven from the heat. Let it cool for a few minutes before serving.
11. Garnish the Campfire Dutch Oven Lasagna with fresh basil leaves, if desired, and serve hot.

Enjoy this delicious and satisfying campfire meal with your fellow outdoor enthusiasts!

Spicy Shrimp and Sausage Skewers

Ingredients:

- 1 lb large shrimp, peeled and deveined
- 1 lb spicy sausage (such as andouille or chorizo), sliced into chunks
- 2 tablespoons olive oil
- 2 cloves garlic, minced
- 1 teaspoon paprika
- 1/2 teaspoon cayenne pepper (adjust to taste)
- 1/2 teaspoon dried thyme
- Salt and pepper to taste
- Wooden skewers, soaked in water for at least 30 minutes

Instructions:

1. Preheat your grill to medium-high heat.
2. In a bowl, combine the olive oil, minced garlic, paprika, cayenne pepper, dried thyme, salt, and pepper. Stir well to make a marinade.
3. Add the peeled and deveined shrimp to the marinade and toss to coat evenly. Let the shrimp marinate for about 15-20 minutes in the refrigerator.
4. Thread the marinated shrimp and chunks of spicy sausage onto the soaked wooden skewers, alternating between the two ingredients.
5. Once all the skewers are assembled, place them on the preheated grill.
6. Grill the skewers for about 3-4 minutes on each side, or until the shrimp are pink and opaque and the sausage is cooked through and slightly charred.
7. Once the skewers are cooked, remove them from the grill and serve immediately.
8. Enjoy your Spicy Shrimp and Sausage Skewers hot off the grill with your favorite sides, such as rice, grilled vegetables, or a fresh salad.

These skewers are packed with flavor and are sure to be a hit at your next outdoor barbecue or cookout!

Cedar Plank Salmon with Maple Glaze

Ingredients:

- 1 cedar plank (soaked in water for at least 1 hour)
- 1 lb salmon fillet, skin-on
- Salt and pepper to taste
- 1/4 cup maple syrup
- 2 tablespoons soy sauce or tamari sauce (for gluten-free option)
- 1 tablespoon Dijon mustard
- 1 tablespoon olive oil
- 2 cloves garlic, minced
- 1 teaspoon grated fresh ginger
- Lemon wedges for serving
- Chopped fresh parsley or green onions for garnish (optional)

Instructions:

1. Preheat your grill to medium-high heat, around 350-400°F (175-200°C).
2. In a small bowl, mix together the maple syrup, soy sauce or tamari sauce, Dijon mustard, olive oil, minced garlic, and grated fresh ginger to make the glaze.
3. Season the salmon fillet with salt and pepper on both sides.
4. Place the soaked cedar plank on the preheated grill and let it heat up for a few minutes until it starts to smoke slightly.
5. Carefully place the seasoned salmon fillet, skin-side down, on the hot cedar plank.
6. Brush the maple glaze generously over the top of the salmon fillet.
7. Close the lid of the grill and let the salmon cook for about 15-20 minutes, or until it flakes easily with a fork and reaches an internal temperature of 145°F (63°C).
8. While the salmon is cooking, occasionally brush more of the maple glaze over the top of the fillet to keep it moist and flavorful.
9. Once the salmon is cooked through, carefully remove it from the grill using a spatula and transfer it to a serving platter.
10. Garnish the Cedar Plank Salmon with Maple Glaze with chopped fresh parsley or green onions, if desired. Serve hot with lemon wedges on the side.
11. Enjoy your delicious and aromatic Cedar Plank Salmon with Maple Glaze as a main course for a memorable outdoor meal.

This dish pairs perfectly with a side of grilled vegetables or a fresh salad.

Campfire Pizza with Fresh Mozzarella and Basil

Ingredients:

- Pizza dough (store-bought or homemade)
- Olive oil, for brushing
- 1 cup marinara sauce
- 8 oz fresh mozzarella cheese, sliced
- Fresh basil leaves
- Salt and pepper to taste
- Optional toppings: sliced tomatoes, olives, mushrooms, peppers, etc.

Instructions:

1. Prepare your campfire by building a medium-sized fire and allowing it to burn down until you have hot coals.
2. While the fire is burning down, roll out the pizza dough on a floured surface to your desired thickness. Shape it into a round or rectangular shape, depending on your preference.
3. Brush one side of the pizza dough with olive oil.
4. Place the oiled side of the pizza dough directly onto a well-oiled grill grate over the hot coals. Cook for about 2-3 minutes, or until the bottom is lightly charred and starting to crisp up.
5. Carefully flip the pizza dough over using tongs or a spatula.
6. Spread marinara sauce evenly over the cooked side of the pizza dough, leaving a small border around the edges.
7. Arrange slices of fresh mozzarella cheese over the marinara sauce.
8. Scatter fresh basil leaves over the mozzarella cheese.
9. Season the pizza with salt and pepper to taste.
10. If desired, add any additional toppings of your choice, such as sliced tomatoes, olives, mushrooms, or peppers.
11. Cover the grill with a lid or aluminum foil and let the pizza cook for another 5-7 minutes, or until the cheese is melted and bubbly and the crust is cooked through.
12. Once the pizza is cooked to your liking, carefully remove it from the grill using a spatula and transfer it to a cutting board.
13. Let the Campfire Pizza with Fresh Mozzarella and Basil cool for a minute or two before slicing it into pieces.
14. Serve hot and enjoy your delicious campfire-cooked pizza under the stars!

Feel free to get creative with your toppings and customize the pizza to suit your tastes. Enjoy your outdoor cooking adventure!

Stuffed Bell Peppers with Ground Turkey and Quinoa

Ingredients:

- 4 large bell peppers, any color
- 1 lb ground turkey
- 1 cup cooked quinoa
- 1 small onion, finely chopped
- 2 cloves garlic, minced
- 1 can (14.5 oz) diced tomatoes, drained
- 1 cup shredded mozzarella cheese
- 1 teaspoon dried oregano
- 1 teaspoon dried basil
- Salt and pepper to taste
- Olive oil for cooking
- Chopped fresh parsley for garnish (optional)

Instructions:

1. Preheat your campfire or grill to medium-high heat.
2. Cut the tops off the bell peppers and remove the seeds and membranes from the inside. Set aside.
3. In a large skillet, heat a drizzle of olive oil over medium heat. Add the chopped onion and minced garlic, and cook until softened and fragrant, about 3-4 minutes.
4. Add the ground turkey to the skillet and cook, breaking it up with a spoon, until browned and cooked through, about 5-6 minutes.
5. Stir in the cooked quinoa, diced tomatoes, dried oregano, dried basil, salt, and pepper. Cook for another 2-3 minutes to allow the flavors to meld together.
6. Remove the skillet from the heat and stir in half of the shredded mozzarella cheese until melted and combined with the turkey mixture.
7. Stuff the bell peppers with the turkey and quinoa mixture, pressing down gently to pack it in.
8. Place the stuffed bell peppers on a grill-safe pan or directly onto the grill grates, ensuring they are stable and won't tip over.
9. Cover the grill with a lid or aluminum foil and let the stuffed bell peppers cook for about 20-25 minutes, or until the peppers are tender and the filling is heated through.
10. During the last few minutes of cooking, sprinkle the remaining shredded mozzarella cheese over the tops of the stuffed bell peppers and let it melt.

11. Once the cheese is melted and bubbly, carefully remove the stuffed bell peppers from the grill using a spatula.
12. Garnish the Stuffed Bell Peppers with Ground Turkey and Quinoa with chopped fresh parsley, if desired, and serve hot.

Enjoy these delicious and nutritious stuffed bell peppers as a wholesome meal during your outdoor adventures!

Foil Packet Cajun Chicken and Vegetables

Ingredients:

- 4 boneless, skinless chicken breasts
- 2 bell peppers, sliced
- 1 red onion, sliced
- 2 zucchinis, sliced
- 2 tablespoons Cajun seasoning
- 2 tablespoons olive oil
- Salt and pepper to taste
- Lemon wedges for serving
- Chopped fresh parsley for garnish (optional)

Instructions:

1. Preheat your grill to medium-high heat.
2. Tear off four large pieces of aluminum foil, each about 12x18 inches in size.
3. Place a chicken breast in the center of each piece of foil.
4. In a bowl, toss together the sliced bell peppers, red onion, and zucchini with Cajun seasoning, olive oil, salt, and pepper until well coated.
5. Divide the seasoned vegetables evenly among the foil packets, placing them on top of the chicken breasts.
6. Fold the sides of each foil packet over the chicken and vegetables, then fold up the ends to seal, creating a tight packet.
7. Place the foil packets on the preheated grill and cook for about 15-20 minutes, or until the chicken is cooked through and the vegetables are tender.
8. Carefully open the foil packets, being cautious of the steam.
9. Serve the Cajun Chicken and Vegetables hot, garnished with chopped fresh parsley and lemon wedges on the side for squeezing over the top.
10. Enjoy your flavorful and hassle-free Foil Packet Cajun Chicken and Vegetables straight from the grill!

This dish is not only delicious but also makes cleanup a breeze, as there are no pots or pans to wash afterward. Perfect for outdoor dining and camping trips!

Grilled Veggie Quesadillas with Avocado Cream

Ingredients:

For the Quesadillas:

- 4 large flour tortillas
- 1 cup shredded Monterey Jack cheese
- 1 cup shredded cheddar cheese
- 1 red bell pepper, thinly sliced
- 1 yellow bell pepper, thinly sliced
- 1 red onion, thinly sliced
- 1 zucchini, thinly sliced
- 1 tablespoon olive oil
- Salt and pepper to taste

For the Avocado Cream:

- 1 ripe avocado
- 1/4 cup sour cream or Greek yogurt
- 1 clove garlic, minced
- 1 tablespoon lime juice
- Salt and pepper to taste

Optional toppings:

- Chopped fresh cilantro
- Sliced jalapenos
- Salsa
- Guacamole

Instructions:

1. Preheat your grill to medium-high heat.
2. In a bowl, toss together the sliced red bell pepper, yellow bell pepper, red onion, and zucchini with olive oil, salt, and pepper until well coated.

3. Place the seasoned vegetables on the preheated grill and cook for about 5-7 minutes, or until they are tender and slightly charred, flipping halfway through cooking.
4. While the vegetables are grilling, make the avocado cream. In a small bowl, mash the ripe avocado with a fork until smooth. Stir in the sour cream or Greek yogurt, minced garlic, lime juice, salt, and pepper until well combined. Set aside.
5. Once the vegetables are cooked, remove them from the grill and set aside.
6. Place a flour tortilla on a clean work surface. Sprinkle shredded Monterey Jack cheese and cheddar cheese evenly over one half of the tortilla.
7. Arrange some of the grilled vegetables over the cheese, then fold the tortilla in half to enclose the filling.
8. Repeat the process with the remaining tortillas and filling ingredients.
9. Place the assembled quesadillas on the preheated grill and cook for about 2-3 minutes on each side, or until the tortillas are crispy and golden brown and the cheese is melted.
10. Once the quesadillas are cooked, remove them from the grill and let them cool for a minute or two before slicing them into wedges.
11. Serve the Grilled Veggie Quesadillas with Avocado Cream hot, garnished with chopped fresh cilantro and sliced jalapenos if desired. Serve with salsa and guacamole on the side for dipping.
12. Enjoy your delicious and flavorful grilled quesadillas as a tasty outdoor meal!

These quesadillas are versatile, so feel free to customize them with your favorite vegetables and toppings.

Campfire Jambalaya with Andouille Sausage and Shrimp

Ingredients:

- 1 lb large shrimp, peeled and deveined
- 1 lb Andouille sausage, sliced
- 1 onion, chopped
- 1 bell pepper, chopped
- 2 stalks celery, chopped
- 3 cloves garlic, minced
- 1 can (14.5 oz) diced tomatoes, undrained
- 1 cup long-grain white rice
- 2 cups chicken broth
- 2 tablespoons Cajun seasoning
- 1 teaspoon dried thyme
- 1 teaspoon dried oregano
- Salt and pepper to taste
- Chopped fresh parsley for garnish (optional)

Instructions:

1. Prepare your campfire by setting up a sturdy cooking grate over the flames.
2. In a large cast iron Dutch oven or skillet, heat a drizzle of oil over the campfire.
3. Add the sliced Andouille sausage to the Dutch oven and cook until browned, about 5-7 minutes.
4. Add the chopped onion, bell pepper, and celery to the Dutch oven with the sausage. Cook until the vegetables are softened, about 5 minutes.
5. Stir in the minced garlic and cook for another minute until fragrant.
6. Add the diced tomatoes (with their juices), long-grain white rice, chicken broth, Cajun seasoning, dried thyme, dried oregano, salt, and pepper to the Dutch oven. Stir well to combine.
7. Bring the mixture to a boil, then reduce the heat to low. Cover the Dutch oven with a lid and let the jambalaya simmer for about 20-25 minutes, or until the rice is cooked and the liquid is absorbed, stirring occasionally.
8. Once the rice is cooked, add the peeled and deveined shrimp to the Dutch oven. Stir well to combine.
9. Cover the Dutch oven again and let the jambalaya cook for an additional 5-7 minutes, or until the shrimp are pink and opaque.
10. Once the shrimp are cooked through, remove the Dutch oven from the heat.

11. Garnish the Campfire Jambalaya with Andouille Sausage and Shrimp with chopped fresh parsley, if desired.
12. Serve hot and enjoy your flavorful and hearty campfire jambalaya straight from the Dutch oven!

This dish is packed with bold Cajun flavors and is sure to be a hit at your next outdoor gathering or camping trip.

Grilled Portobello Mushrooms Stuffed with Goat Cheese and Spinach

Ingredients:

- 4 large Portobello mushrooms, stems removed
- 2 tablespoons olive oil
- Salt and pepper to taste
- 4 oz fresh baby spinach
- 4 oz goat cheese, crumbled
- 2 cloves garlic, minced
- 1/4 cup grated Parmesan cheese
- Fresh basil leaves for garnish (optional)

Instructions:

1. Preheat your grill to medium-high heat.
2. Clean the Portobello mushrooms by wiping them with a damp paper towel to remove any dirt. Remove the stems and discard them.
3. Brush both sides of the Portobello mushrooms with olive oil and season them with salt and pepper to taste.
4. In a skillet, heat a drizzle of olive oil over medium heat. Add the minced garlic and cook for about 1 minute until fragrant.
5. Add the fresh baby spinach to the skillet and cook, stirring occasionally, until wilted, about 2-3 minutes.
6. Remove the skillet from the heat and let the spinach cool slightly.
7. In a bowl, combine the cooked spinach with crumbled goat cheese and grated Parmesan cheese. Mix well to combine.
8. Spoon the spinach and goat cheese mixture evenly into the cavity of each Portobello mushroom, pressing it down gently to fill.
9. Place the stuffed Portobello mushrooms on the preheated grill, gill-side down.
10. Grill the mushrooms for about 5-7 minutes on each side, or until they are tender and the cheese is melted and slightly browned.
11. Once the mushrooms are cooked through, carefully remove them from the grill using a spatula.
12. Garnish the Grilled Portobello Mushrooms Stuffed with Goat Cheese and Spinach with fresh basil leaves, if desired.
13. Serve hot as a delicious appetizer or main course.

These stuffed Portobello mushrooms are bursting with flavor and are sure to impress your guests at your next outdoor gathering or barbecue! Enjoy!

Campfire Beef and Bean Chili

Ingredients:

- 1 lb ground beef
- 1 onion, chopped
- 3 cloves garlic, minced
- 1 bell pepper, diced
- 1 can (15 oz) kidney beans, drained and rinsed
- 1 can (15 oz) black beans, drained and rinsed
- 1 can (14.5 oz) diced tomatoes, undrained
- 1 can (6 oz) tomato paste
- 2 cups beef broth
- 2 tablespoons chili powder
- 1 teaspoon ground cumin
- 1 teaspoon smoked paprika
- Salt and pepper to taste
- Optional toppings: shredded cheddar cheese, sour cream, chopped green onions, sliced jalapenos, chopped cilantro

Instructions:

1. Heat a large cast iron Dutch oven over the campfire or on a grill grate.
2. Add the ground beef to the Dutch oven and cook, breaking it up with a spoon, until browned and cooked through.
3. Add the chopped onion, minced garlic, and diced bell pepper to the Dutch oven with the cooked ground beef. Cook until the vegetables are softened, about 5 minutes.
4. Stir in the drained and rinsed kidney beans, black beans, diced tomatoes, tomato paste, beef broth, chili powder, ground cumin, smoked paprika, salt, and pepper.
5. Bring the chili to a simmer, then reduce the heat to low. Cover the Dutch oven with a lid and let the chili cook for about 30-40 minutes, stirring occasionally, to allow the flavors to meld together and the chili to thicken.
6. Taste the chili and adjust the seasoning with salt and pepper if needed.
7. Once the chili is cooked to your liking and has thickened to your desired consistency, remove it from the heat.
8. Serve the Campfire Beef and Bean Chili hot, garnished with your favorite toppings such as shredded cheddar cheese, sour cream, chopped green onions, sliced jalapenos, and chopped cilantro.

9. Enjoy your delicious and comforting campfire chili on a cool evening under the stars!

This chili is perfect for serving with cornbread, crackers, or even over baked potatoes for a hearty meal.

Lemon Herb Chicken Skewers with Greek Yogurt Sauce

Ingredients:

For the Chicken Skewers:

- 1.5 lbs boneless, skinless chicken breasts, cut into 1-inch cubes
- 2 tablespoons olive oil
- Zest of 1 lemon
- Juice of 1 lemon
- 2 cloves garlic, minced
- 1 teaspoon dried oregano
- 1 teaspoon dried thyme
- Salt and pepper to taste
- Wooden skewers, soaked in water for at least 30 minutes

For the Greek Yogurt Sauce:

- 1 cup Greek yogurt
- 1/4 cup chopped fresh dill
- 1/4 cup chopped fresh parsley
- 1 tablespoon lemon juice
- 1 clove garlic, minced
- Salt and pepper to taste

Instructions:

1. In a bowl, combine the olive oil, lemon zest, lemon juice, minced garlic, dried oregano, dried thyme, salt, and pepper to make the marinade for the chicken.
2. Add the chicken cubes to the marinade and toss to coat evenly. Cover the bowl and let the chicken marinate in the refrigerator for at least 30 minutes, or up to 2 hours.
3. While the chicken is marinating, prepare the Greek yogurt sauce. In a bowl, combine the Greek yogurt, chopped fresh dill, chopped fresh parsley, lemon juice, minced garlic, salt, and pepper. Stir well to combine. Cover the bowl and refrigerate until ready to serve.
4. Preheat your grill to medium-high heat.

5. Thread the marinated chicken cubes onto the soaked wooden skewers, dividing them evenly among the skewers.
6. Once the grill is hot, place the chicken skewers on the grill grates. Cook for about 8-10 minutes, turning occasionally, until the chicken is cooked through and nicely charred on all sides.
7. Once the chicken skewers are cooked, remove them from the grill and let them rest for a few minutes.
8. Serve the Lemon Herb Chicken Skewers hot, with the Greek yogurt sauce on the side for dipping.
9. Enjoy your flavorful and refreshing chicken skewers with the tangy Greek yogurt sauce!

These skewers pair well with a side of grilled vegetables, rice, or a fresh salad for a complete and satisfying meal.

Foil Packet Garlic Butter Shrimp

Ingredients:

- 1 lb large shrimp, peeled and deveined
- 4 cloves garlic, minced
- 1/4 cup unsalted butter, melted
- 2 tablespoons fresh lemon juice
- 1 tablespoon chopped fresh parsley
- Salt and pepper to taste
- Lemon slices for garnish
- Chopped fresh parsley for garnish

Instructions:

1. Preheat your grill to medium-high heat.
2. In a bowl, combine the minced garlic, melted butter, fresh lemon juice, chopped parsley, salt, and pepper. Mix well to make the garlic butter sauce.
3. Tear off four large pieces of aluminum foil, each about 12x18 inches in size.
4. Divide the peeled and deveined shrimp evenly among the foil packets, placing them in the center of each piece of foil.
5. Pour the garlic butter sauce evenly over the shrimp in each foil packet.
6. Fold the sides of each foil packet over the shrimp to cover them completely, then fold up the ends to seal, creating a tight packet.
7. Place the foil packets on the preheated grill and cook for about 8-10 minutes, or until the shrimp are pink and opaque, and the garlic butter sauce is bubbling.
8. Carefully open the foil packets, being cautious of the steam.
9. Transfer the garlic butter shrimp to serving plates or a platter. Garnish with lemon slices and chopped fresh parsley.
10. Serve hot and enjoy your delicious Foil Packet Garlic Butter Shrimp straight from the grill!

These shrimp are bursting with flavor and are perfect for serving as an appetizer or main course at your next outdoor gathering or barbecue. Enjoy!

Grilled Halibut Tacos with Mango Salsa

Ingredients:

For the Grilled Halibut:

- 1 lb halibut fillets
- 2 tablespoons olive oil
- 1 teaspoon chili powder
- 1/2 teaspoon ground cumin
- 1/2 teaspoon garlic powder
- Salt and pepper to taste
- 8 small corn or flour tortillas

For the Mango Salsa:

- 1 ripe mango, diced
- 1/2 red onion, finely chopped
- 1/2 red bell pepper, diced
- 1/4 cup chopped fresh cilantro
- Juice of 1 lime
- Salt and pepper to taste

For Serving:

- Shredded cabbage or lettuce
- Sliced avocado
- Sour cream or Greek yogurt
- Lime wedges

Instructions:

1. Preheat your grill to medium-high heat.
2. In a small bowl, mix together the olive oil, chili powder, ground cumin, garlic powder, salt, and pepper to make a marinade for the halibut.

3. Pat the halibut fillets dry with paper towels. Brush both sides of the halibut fillets with the marinade.
4. Place the halibut fillets on the preheated grill. Grill for about 4-5 minutes per side, or until the fish is cooked through and flakes easily with a fork.
5. While the halibut is grilling, prepare the mango salsa. In a bowl, combine the diced mango, finely chopped red onion, diced red bell pepper, chopped fresh cilantro, lime juice, salt, and pepper. Stir well to combine.
6. Warm the tortillas on the grill for about 30 seconds on each side, or until they are heated through and slightly charred.
7. Once the halibut is cooked, remove it from the grill and let it rest for a few minutes. Then, use a fork to flake the halibut into bite-sized pieces.
8. To assemble the tacos, place some shredded cabbage or lettuce on each tortilla. Top with the grilled halibut pieces, mango salsa, sliced avocado, and a dollop of sour cream or Greek yogurt.
9. Serve the Grilled Halibut Tacos with Mango Salsa hot, with lime wedges on the side for squeezing over the top.
10. Enjoy your fresh and flavorful halibut tacos as a delicious outdoor meal!

These tacos are bursting with tropical flavors and are sure to be a hit at your next outdoor gathering or barbecue.

Campfire Paella with Chorizo and Seafood

Ingredients:

- 1 lb large shrimp, peeled and deveined
- 1 lb mussels, cleaned and debearded
- 1 lb clams, cleaned
- 8 oz Spanish chorizo, sliced
- 1 onion, chopped
- 3 cloves garlic, minced
- 1 red bell pepper, diced
- 1 yellow bell pepper, diced
- 1 cup Arborio rice
- 1 can (14.5 oz) diced tomatoes, undrained
- 3 cups chicken broth
- 1 teaspoon smoked paprika
- 1 teaspoon saffron threads (optional)
- Salt and pepper to taste
- Olive oil for cooking
- Lemon wedges for serving
- Chopped fresh parsley for garnish

Instructions:

1. Prepare your campfire by setting up a stable cooking area with a grill grate over hot coals.
2. In a large cast iron skillet or Dutch oven, heat a drizzle of olive oil over the campfire.
3. Add the sliced chorizo to the skillet and cook until browned and slightly crispy, about 3-4 minutes.
4. Add the chopped onion, minced garlic, diced red bell pepper, and diced yellow bell pepper to the skillet with the chorizo. Cook until the vegetables are softened, about 5 minutes.
5. Stir in the Arborio rice and cook for another 2-3 minutes, stirring occasionally, until the rice is lightly toasted.
6. Pour in the diced tomatoes (with their juices) and chicken broth. Add the smoked paprika and saffron threads, if using. Stir well to combine.

7. Bring the mixture to a simmer. Cover the skillet or Dutch oven with a lid and let the paella cook for about 15-20 minutes, or until the rice is almost tender and most of the liquid has been absorbed, stirring occasionally.
8. Once the rice is almost cooked, arrange the peeled and deveined shrimp, cleaned mussels, and cleaned clams on top of the paella. Cover the skillet or Dutch oven again and let the seafood cook for another 5-7 minutes, or until the shrimp are pink and opaque and the mussels and clams have opened.
9. Discard any mussels or clams that have not opened.
10. Once the seafood is cooked through, remove the skillet or Dutch oven from the heat.
11. Garnish the Campfire Paella with Chorizo and Seafood with chopped fresh parsley and serve hot, with lemon wedges on the side for squeezing over the top.
12. Enjoy your flavorful and aromatic paella straight from the campfire!

This paella is perfect for serving as a main course at outdoor gatherings or camping trips. It's sure to impress your friends and family with its bold flavors and beautiful presentation.

BBQ Pulled Pork Stuffed Sweet Potatoes

Ingredients:

For the BBQ Pulled Pork:

- 2 lbs pork shoulder or pork butt
- 1 cup BBQ sauce (homemade or store-bought)
- 1/2 cup chicken broth
- 1 tablespoon olive oil
- 1 onion, diced
- 3 cloves garlic, minced
- Salt and pepper to taste

For the Sweet Potatoes:

- 4 medium-sized sweet potatoes
- Olive oil for brushing
- Salt and pepper to taste

Optional Toppings:

- Chopped green onions
- Chopped cilantro
- Shredded cheddar cheese
- Sour cream or Greek yogurt

Instructions:

For the BBQ Pulled Pork:

1. Preheat your grill or smoker to 225°F (107°C).
2. Season the pork shoulder or pork butt with salt and pepper.
3. In a large skillet, heat the olive oil over medium heat. Add the diced onion and minced garlic, and cook until softened and fragrant, about 5 minutes.

4. Place the seasoned pork shoulder or pork butt directly on the grill or smoker. Close the lid and let it smoke for about 4-5 hours, or until it reaches an internal temperature of 195-200°F (90-93°C) and is tender enough to shred with a fork.
5. In a small bowl, mix together the BBQ sauce and chicken broth.
6. Once the pork is cooked, transfer it to a cutting board and let it rest for a few minutes. Then, shred the meat using two forks.
7. Place the shredded pork back into the skillet with the cooked onions and garlic. Pour the BBQ sauce mixture over the shredded pork and stir to combine.
8. Cook the BBQ pulled pork mixture over medium heat for another 5-10 minutes, stirring occasionally, until heated through and the flavors are well combined.

For the Sweet Potatoes:

1. Preheat your grill to medium-high heat.
2. Pierce each sweet potato several times with a fork.
3. Brush the sweet potatoes with olive oil and sprinkle them with salt and pepper.
4. Place the sweet potatoes directly on the grill grates and close the lid. Grill for about 45-60 minutes, or until the sweet potatoes are tender and cooked through, turning occasionally to ensure even cooking.

Assembly:

1. Once the sweet potatoes are cooked, remove them from the grill and let them cool slightly.
2. Slice each sweet potato lengthwise down the center, leaving the ends intact.
3. Use a fork to fluff the insides of each sweet potato.
4. Spoon the BBQ pulled pork mixture generously into each sweet potato.
5. Top the stuffed sweet potatoes with your desired toppings, such as chopped green onions, chopped cilantro, shredded cheddar cheese, and sour cream or Greek yogurt.
6. Serve immediately and enjoy your BBQ Pulled Pork Stuffed Sweet Potatoes!

These stuffed sweet potatoes are a crowd-pleaser and are perfect for serving at gatherings or for a cozy weeknight meal.

Grilled Zucchini Ribbons with Pesto

Ingredients:

For the Pesto:

- 2 cups fresh basil leaves, packed
- 1/3 cup pine nuts or walnuts
- 3 cloves garlic, peeled
- 1/2 cup grated Parmesan cheese
- 1/2 cup extra-virgin olive oil
- Salt and pepper to taste

For the Zucchini Ribbons:

- 3-4 medium-sized zucchini
- Olive oil for brushing
- Salt and pepper to taste
- Grated Parmesan cheese for garnish (optional)

Instructions:

For the Pesto:

1. In a food processor, combine the basil leaves, pine nuts or walnuts, and garlic cloves. Pulse until coarsely chopped.
2. Add the grated Parmesan cheese to the food processor. With the motor running, slowly pour in the olive oil in a steady stream. Continue processing until the pesto reaches your desired consistency.
3. Season the pesto with salt and pepper to taste. Transfer it to a bowl and set aside.

For the Zucchini Ribbons:

1. Preheat your grill to medium-high heat.
2. Using a vegetable peeler or a mandoline slicer, slice the zucchini lengthwise into thin ribbons.

3. Brush both sides of the zucchini ribbons with olive oil and season them with salt and pepper.
4. Place the zucchini ribbons directly on the preheated grill. Grill for about 1-2 minutes per side, or until they are lightly charred and tender.
5. Once the zucchini ribbons are grilled, transfer them to a serving platter or individual plates.
6. Drizzle the grilled zucchini ribbons with the prepared pesto, using as much or as little as you like.
7. If desired, sprinkle some grated Parmesan cheese over the top for extra flavor.
8. Serve the Grilled Zucchini Ribbons with Pesto immediately as a delicious and light side dish.

These grilled zucchini ribbons with pesto are a wonderful way to showcase the flavors of summer produce. They're perfect for serving alongside grilled meats or as part of a vegetarian meal. Enjoy!

Foil Packet Lemon Garlic Chicken with Asparagus

Ingredients:

- 4 boneless, skinless chicken breasts
- 1 lb fresh asparagus, trimmed
- 4 cloves garlic, minced
- Zest of 1 lemon
- Juice of 1 lemon
- 4 tablespoons unsalted butter, melted
- Salt and pepper to taste
- Fresh parsley for garnish (optional)

Instructions:

1. Preheat your grill to medium-high heat.
2. Tear off four large pieces of aluminum foil, each about 12x18 inches in size.
3. Season both sides of the chicken breasts with salt and pepper to taste.
4. Place one chicken breast in the center of each piece of foil.
5. Divide the trimmed asparagus evenly among the foil packets, placing them next to the chicken breasts.
6. In a small bowl, whisk together the minced garlic, lemon zest, lemon juice, and melted butter.
7. Pour the lemon garlic butter mixture evenly over the chicken breasts and asparagus in each foil packet.
8. Fold the sides of each foil packet over the chicken and asparagus to cover them completely, then fold up the ends to seal, creating a tight packet.
9. Place the foil packets on the preheated grill and cook for about 15-20 minutes, or until the chicken is cooked through and reaches an internal temperature of 165°F (75°C), and the asparagus is tender.
10. Carefully open the foil packets, being cautious of the steam.
11. Transfer the chicken breasts and asparagus to serving plates or a platter.
12. Garnish the Foil Packet Lemon Garlic Chicken with Asparagus with chopped fresh parsley, if desired.
13. Serve hot and enjoy your delicious and flavorful chicken and asparagus straight from the grill!

This dish is not only easy to make but also results in tender and juicy chicken with bright, citrusy flavors. It's perfect for a quick and satisfying outdoor meal.

Campfire Ratatouille with Fresh Herbs

Ingredients:

- 4 boneless, skinless chicken breasts
- 1 lb fresh asparagus, trimmed
- 4 cloves garlic, minced
- Zest of 1 lemon
- Juice of 1 lemon
- 4 tablespoons unsalted butter, melted
- Salt and pepper to taste
- Fresh parsley for garnish (optional)

Instructions:

1. Preheat your grill to medium-high heat.
2. Tear off four large pieces of aluminum foil, each about 12x18 inches in size.
3. Season both sides of the chicken breasts with salt and pepper to taste.
4. Place one chicken breast in the center of each piece of foil.
5. Divide the trimmed asparagus evenly among the foil packets, placing them next to the chicken breasts.
6. In a small bowl, whisk together the minced garlic, lemon zest, lemon juice, and melted butter.
7. Pour the lemon garlic butter mixture evenly over the chicken breasts and asparagus in each foil packet.
8. Fold the sides of each foil packet over the chicken and asparagus to cover them completely, then fold up the ends to seal, creating a tight packet.
9. Place the foil packets on the preheated grill and cook for about 15-20 minutes, or until the chicken is cooked through and reaches an internal temperature of 165°F (75°C), and the asparagus is tender.
10. Carefully open the foil packets, being cautious of the steam.
11. Transfer the chicken breasts and asparagus to serving plates or a platter.
12. Garnish the Foil Packet Lemon Garlic Chicken with Asparagus with chopped fresh parsley, if desired.
13. Serve hot and enjoy your delicious and flavorful chicken and asparagus straight from the grill!

This dish is not only easy to make but also results in tender and juicy chicken with bright, citrusy flavors. It's perfect for a quick and satisfying outdoor meal.

Grilled Swordfish Steaks with Tomato Basil Relish

Ingredients:

For the Swordfish Steaks:

- 4 swordfish steaks (about 6 ounces each)
- 2 tablespoons olive oil
- Salt and pepper to taste
- Lemon wedges for serving

For the Tomato Basil Relish:

- 2 cups cherry tomatoes, halved
- 1/4 cup chopped fresh basil
- 2 tablespoons chopped red onion
- 1 tablespoon balsamic vinegar
- 1 tablespoon olive oil
- Salt and pepper to taste

Instructions:

For the Swordfish Steaks:

1. Preheat your grill to medium-high heat.
2. Pat the swordfish steaks dry with paper towels and brush them lightly with olive oil.
3. Season both sides of the swordfish steaks with salt and pepper to taste.
4. Place the swordfish steaks on the preheated grill and cook for about 4-5 minutes per side, or until they are cooked through and have grill marks. The internal temperature of the swordfish should reach 145°F (63°C).
5. Once the swordfish steaks are cooked, remove them from the grill and let them rest for a few minutes.

For the Tomato Basil Relish:

1. In a bowl, combine the halved cherry tomatoes, chopped fresh basil, chopped red onion, balsamic vinegar, olive oil, salt, and pepper. Stir well to combine.
2. Taste the tomato basil relish and adjust the seasoning with salt and pepper if needed.

Assembly:

1. Place the grilled swordfish steaks on serving plates.
2. Spoon the tomato basil relish over the top of each swordfish steak.
3. Garnish with additional fresh basil leaves, if desired, and serve with lemon wedges on the side.
4. Enjoy your Grilled Swordfish Steaks with Tomato Basil Relish as a delicious and elegant summer meal!

This dish pairs beautifully with a side of grilled vegetables, rice, or a fresh salad. The bright and flavorful tomato basil relish complements the rich and meaty swordfish steaks perfectly.

Sweet and Spicy Korean BBQ Chicken Skewers

Ingredients:

For the Chicken Marinade:

- 1.5 lbs boneless, skinless chicken thighs, cut into bite-sized pieces
- 1/4 cup soy sauce
- 2 tablespoons honey or maple syrup
- 2 tablespoons gochujang (Korean chili paste)
- 2 tablespoons sesame oil
- 2 cloves garlic, minced
- 1 tablespoon grated ginger
- 1 tablespoon rice vinegar
- 1 tablespoon brown sugar
- 1 teaspoon sesame seeds (optional)
- Salt and pepper to taste

For the Skewers:

- Wooden skewers, soaked in water for at least 30 minutes

For Garnish:

- Thinly sliced green onions
- Sesame seeds

Instructions:

1. In a bowl, combine the soy sauce, honey or maple syrup, gochujang, sesame oil, minced garlic, grated ginger, rice vinegar, brown sugar, sesame seeds (if using), salt, and pepper to make the marinade.
2. Add the bite-sized chicken thigh pieces to the marinade and toss until evenly coated. Cover the bowl and let the chicken marinate in the refrigerator for at least 30 minutes, or up to 4 hours.
3. Preheat your grill to medium-high heat.

4. Thread the marinated chicken pieces onto the soaked wooden skewers, dividing them evenly among the skewers.
5. Once the grill is hot, place the chicken skewers on the grill grates. Cook for about 5-6 minutes on each side, or until the chicken is cooked through and has nice grill marks.
6. While the chicken skewers are cooking, you can brush them with any remaining marinade for extra flavor, if desired.
7. Once the chicken skewers are cooked through, remove them from the grill and transfer them to a serving platter.
8. Garnish the Sweet and Spicy Korean BBQ Chicken Skewers with thinly sliced green onions and sesame seeds.
9. Serve hot and enjoy your flavorful and delicious chicken skewers straight from the grill!

These Sweet and Spicy Korean BBQ Chicken Skewers are perfect for serving as an appetizer or main course at your next barbecue or gathering. The combination of sweet, savory, and spicy flavors is sure to be a hit with everyone!

Campfire Beef Stroganoff with Mushrooms

Ingredients:

- 1 lb beef sirloin or tenderloin, thinly sliced
- 8 oz mushrooms, sliced
- 1 onion, finely chopped
- 2 cloves garlic, minced
- 2 tablespoons butter
- 2 tablespoons all-purpose flour
- 1 cup beef broth
- 1/2 cup sour cream
- 2 tablespoons Worcestershire sauce
- Salt and pepper to taste
- Cooked egg noodles or rice for serving
- Chopped fresh parsley for garnish (optional)

Instructions:

1. Heat a large cast iron skillet or Dutch oven over the campfire or on a grill grate.
2. Add the sliced beef to the skillet and cook until browned on all sides, about 5-7 minutes. Remove the beef from the skillet and set it aside.
3. In the same skillet, add the butter, sliced mushrooms, chopped onion, and minced garlic. Cook until the vegetables are softened, about 5 minutes.
4. Sprinkle the flour over the mushrooms and onions in the skillet. Stir well to combine and cook for another 1-2 minutes to cook off the raw flour taste.
5. Slowly pour the beef broth into the skillet, stirring constantly to prevent lumps from forming. Cook until the sauce thickens, about 3-5 minutes.
6. Stir in the sour cream and Worcestershire sauce until well combined.
7. Return the cooked beef to the skillet and stir to coat it with the sauce. Season with salt and pepper to taste.
8. Let the beef stroganoff simmer over the campfire for another 5-7 minutes, stirring occasionally, to allow the flavors to meld together.
9. Once the beef stroganoff is heated through and the sauce has thickened to your desired consistency, remove the skillet from the heat.
10. Serve the Campfire Beef Stroganoff with Mushrooms hot, spooned over cooked egg noodles or rice.
11. Garnish with chopped fresh parsley, if desired, and enjoy your hearty and comforting campfire meal!

This dish is perfect for serving at outdoor gatherings or camping trips, and its rich and creamy sauce paired with tender beef and mushrooms is sure to satisfy everyone around the campfire.

Foil Packet Coconut-Lime Shrimp

Ingredients:

- 1 lb large shrimp, peeled and deveined
- 1 bell pepper, thinly sliced
- 1 small onion, thinly sliced
- 1 cup cherry tomatoes, halved
- 1/2 cup unsweetened shredded coconut
- Zest and juice of 1 lime
- 2 tablespoons olive oil
- 2 cloves garlic, minced
- 1 teaspoon ground cumin
- Salt and pepper to taste
- Fresh cilantro for garnish
- Cooked rice or quinoa for serving (optional)

Instructions:

1. Preheat your grill to medium-high heat.
2. Tear off four large pieces of aluminum foil, each about 12x18 inches in size.
3. In a large bowl, combine the peeled and deveined shrimp, thinly sliced bell pepper, thinly sliced onion, halved cherry tomatoes, unsweetened shredded coconut, lime zest, lime juice, olive oil, minced garlic, ground cumin, salt, and pepper. Toss until everything is evenly coated.
4. Divide the shrimp and vegetable mixture evenly among the foil packets, placing it in the center of each piece of foil.
5. Fold the sides of each foil packet over the shrimp and vegetables to cover them completely, then fold up the ends to seal, creating a tight packet.
6. Place the foil packets on the preheated grill and cook for about 10-12 minutes, or until the shrimp are pink and opaque and the vegetables are tender.
7. Carefully open the foil packets, being cautious of the steam.
8. Serve the Foil Packet Coconut-Lime Shrimp hot, garnished with fresh cilantro, and with cooked rice or quinoa on the side, if desired.
9. Enjoy your flavorful and easy coconut-lime shrimp straight from the grill!

These foil packets are not only delicious but also make for easy cleanup, making them perfect for outdoor dining. Serve them as a main course or as part of a larger meal for a delightful taste of summer!

Grilled Eggplant Parmesan Stacks

Ingredients:

- 2 large eggplants, sliced into 1/2-inch rounds
- Olive oil for brushing
- Salt and pepper to taste
- 2 cups marinara sauce
- 1 cup shredded mozzarella cheese
- 1/2 cup grated Parmesan cheese
- Fresh basil leaves for garnish

Instructions:

1. Preheat your grill to medium-high heat.
2. Place the eggplant slices on a baking sheet and brush both sides with olive oil. Season with salt and pepper to taste.
3. Grill the eggplant slices for about 3-4 minutes on each side, or until they are tender and have grill marks.
4. Remove the grilled eggplant slices from the grill and let them cool slightly.
5. Preheat your oven to 375°F (190°C).
6. In a small baking dish or oven-safe skillet, spread a thin layer of marinara sauce on the bottom.
7. Place a grilled eggplant slice on top of the marinara sauce, then add a spoonful of marinara sauce on top of the eggplant slice.
8. Sprinkle some shredded mozzarella cheese and grated Parmesan cheese on top of the marinara sauce.
9. Repeat the layers with the remaining grilled eggplant slices, marinara sauce, and cheeses, stacking them into individual stacks.
10. Bake the eggplant Parmesan stacks in the preheated oven for about 10-12 minutes, or until the cheese is melted and bubbly.
11. Once the cheese is melted and bubbly, remove the eggplant Parmesan stacks from the oven.
12. Garnish the Grilled Eggplant Parmesan Stacks with fresh basil leaves before serving.
13. Serve hot and enjoy your delicious and cheesy eggplant stacks!

These Grilled Eggplant Parmesan Stacks are perfect for serving as a vegetarian main course or as a side dish to accompany grilled meats or seafood. They're bursting with flavor and are sure to be a hit at your next summer gathering!

Campfire Cornbread Stuffed with Jalapenos and Cheddar

Ingredients:

- 1 cup cornmeal
- 1 cup all-purpose flour
- 1/4 cup granulated sugar
- 1 tablespoon baking powder
- 1 teaspoon salt
- 1 cup buttermilk
- 1/2 cup unsalted butter, melted
- 2 eggs
- 1 cup shredded cheddar cheese
- 2-3 jalapeno peppers, seeded and finely chopped

Instructions:

1. Preheat your campfire or grill to medium heat.
2. In a large bowl, whisk together the cornmeal, all-purpose flour, sugar, baking powder, and salt until well combined.
3. In a separate bowl, whisk together the buttermilk, melted butter, and eggs until smooth.
4. Pour the wet ingredients into the dry ingredients and stir until just combined. Be careful not to overmix.
5. Fold in the shredded cheddar cheese and finely chopped jalapeno peppers until evenly distributed throughout the batter.
6. Grease a cast iron skillet or a disposable aluminum baking pan with butter or cooking spray.
7. Pour half of the cornbread batter into the prepared skillet or pan, spreading it out evenly.
8. Spoon the remaining cornbread batter on top, spreading it out to cover the bottom layer.
9. Place the skillet or pan on the campfire grill grate, cover with a lid or foil, and cook for about 20-25 minutes, or until the cornbread is golden brown and a toothpick inserted into the center comes out clean.
10. Once the cornbread is cooked through, remove it from the campfire and let it cool for a few minutes before slicing and serving.
11. Serve the Campfire Cornbread Stuffed with Jalapenos and Cheddar warm as a side dish or snack.

12. Enjoy the delicious combination of savory cheddar cheese and spicy jalapenos in every bite!

This campfire cornbread is perfect for serving alongside grilled meats, chili, or enjoying on its own as a tasty snack. It's sure to be a hit at your next outdoor gathering or camping trip!

Grilled Mahi Mahi Tacos with Pineapple Salsa

Ingredients:

For the Grilled Mahi Mahi:

- 1 lb mahi mahi fillets
- 2 tablespoons olive oil
- Juice of 1 lime
- 1 teaspoon chili powder
- 1 teaspoon ground cumin
- Salt and pepper to taste

For the Pineapple Salsa:

- 1 cup diced pineapple
- 1/2 cup diced red onion
- 1/2 cup diced red bell pepper
- 1/4 cup chopped fresh cilantro
- Juice of 1 lime
- Salt and pepper to taste

For Serving:

- 8 small corn or flour tortillas, warmed
- Shredded cabbage or lettuce
- Sliced avocado
- Sour cream or Greek yogurt
- Lime wedges

Instructions:

For the Grilled Mahi Mahi:

1. Preheat your grill to medium-high heat.

2. In a small bowl, mix together the olive oil, lime juice, chili powder, ground cumin, salt, and pepper to create a marinade.
3. Pat the mahi mahi fillets dry with paper towels and place them in a shallow dish. Pour the marinade over the fillets, turning to coat evenly. Let them marinate for about 15-30 minutes.
4. Once the grill is hot, remove the mahi mahi fillets from the marinade and place them directly on the grill grates. Grill for about 3-4 minutes per side, or until the fish is cooked through and flakes easily with a fork.
5. Remove the grilled mahi mahi from the grill and let it rest for a few minutes. Then, use a fork to flake the fish into bite-sized pieces.

For the Pineapple Salsa:

1. In a medium bowl, combine the diced pineapple, red onion, red bell pepper, chopped cilantro, lime juice, salt, and pepper. Stir well to combine.
2. Taste the salsa and adjust the seasoning if needed with additional salt, pepper, or lime juice.

Assembly:

1. To assemble the tacos, place some shredded cabbage or lettuce on each warmed tortilla.
2. Top with the grilled mahi mahi pieces and spoon the pineapple salsa over the fish.
3. Add sliced avocado on top and a dollop of sour cream or Greek yogurt if desired.
4. Serve the Grilled Mahi Mahi Tacos with Pineapple Salsa hot, with lime wedges on the side for squeezing over the top.
5. Enjoy your delicious and vibrant tacos!

These Grilled Mahi Mahi Tacos with Pineapple Salsa are bursting with fresh flavors and make for a perfect summer meal. They're great for entertaining or for a casual weeknight dinner with family and friends.

Foil Packet Teriyaki Salmon and Veggies

Ingredients:

- 4 salmon fillets
- 2 cups broccoli florets
- 1 red bell pepper, sliced
- 1 yellow bell pepper, sliced
- 1 zucchini, sliced
- 1/2 cup teriyaki sauce
- 2 tablespoons soy sauce
- 2 cloves garlic, minced
- 1 tablespoon grated ginger
- Sesame seeds for garnish (optional)
- Sliced green onions for garnish (optional)

Instructions:

1. Preheat your grill to medium-high heat.
2. Cut four large pieces of aluminum foil, each about 12x18 inches in size.
3. In a small bowl, whisk together the teriyaki sauce, soy sauce, minced garlic, and grated ginger to make the teriyaki marinade.
4. Place one salmon fillet in the center of each piece of foil.
5. Divide the broccoli florets, sliced red bell pepper, sliced yellow bell pepper, and sliced zucchini evenly among the foil packets, arranging them around the salmon fillets.
6. Pour the teriyaki marinade over the salmon and vegetables in each foil packet, making sure everything is evenly coated.
7. Fold the sides of each foil packet over the salmon and vegetables to cover them completely, then fold up the ends to seal, creating a tight packet.
8. Place the foil packets on the preheated grill and cook for about 10-12 minutes, or until the salmon is cooked through and flakes easily with a fork, and the vegetables are tender.
9. Carefully open the foil packets, being cautious of the steam.
10. Transfer the salmon fillets and vegetables to serving plates or a platter.
11. Garnish with sesame seeds and sliced green onions, if desired.
12. Serve hot and enjoy your flavorful and delicious foil packet teriyaki salmon and veggies straight from the grill!

These foil packet teriyaki salmon and veggies are not only easy to make but also result in tender and flavorful salmon with perfectly cooked vegetables. They're perfect for a quick and satisfying outdoor meal.

Campfire Risotto with Wild Mushrooms and Parmesan

Ingredients:

- 1 cup Arborio rice
- 4 cups chicken or vegetable broth
- 1/2 cup white wine (optional)
- 2 tablespoons olive oil
- 1 onion, finely chopped
- 2 cloves garlic, minced
- 8 oz wild mushrooms (such as shiitake, oyster, or chanterelle), sliced
- 1/2 cup grated Parmesan cheese
- Salt and pepper to taste
- Fresh parsley for garnish

Instructions:

1. Heat your campfire grill or outdoor stove to medium heat.
2. In a large skillet or Dutch oven, heat the olive oil over the campfire. Add the chopped onion and minced garlic, and cook until softened and fragrant, about 3-4 minutes.
3. Add the sliced wild mushrooms to the skillet and cook until they release their moisture and start to brown, about 5-6 minutes.
4. Add the Arborio rice to the skillet and stir to coat it with the oil and cook for another 1-2 minutes, allowing the rice to toast slightly.
5. If using, pour in the white wine and cook until it's absorbed by the rice, stirring constantly.
6. Begin adding the chicken or vegetable broth to the skillet, one ladleful at a time, stirring constantly and allowing the liquid to absorb before adding more. Continue this process until the rice is creamy and cooked al dente, about 18-20 minutes.
7. Once the risotto is cooked to your desired consistency, remove the skillet from the heat.
8. Stir in the grated Parmesan cheese until it's melted and well incorporated into the risotto. Season with salt and pepper to taste.
9. Garnish the Campfire Risotto with Wild Mushrooms and Parmesan with fresh parsley before serving.
10. Serve hot and enjoy your delicious and creamy risotto straight from the campfire!

This campfire risotto with wild mushrooms and Parmesan is a comforting and satisfying dish that's perfect for enjoying outdoors on a cool evening. It's creamy, flavorful, and sure to be a hit with everyone around the campfire!

Grilled Thai Beef Salad with Peanut Dressing

Ingredients:

For the Grilled Beef:

- 1 lb flank steak or sirloin steak
- 2 tablespoons soy sauce
- 2 tablespoons fish sauce
- 2 cloves garlic, minced
- 1 tablespoon brown sugar
- 1 teaspoon grated ginger
- 1 teaspoon ground coriander
- 1/2 teaspoon chili flakes (optional)
- Salt and pepper to taste

For the Peanut Dressing:

- 1/4 cup peanut butter
- 2 tablespoons soy sauce
- 2 tablespoons rice vinegar
- 1 tablespoon honey
- 1 tablespoon sesame oil
- 1 clove garlic, minced
- 1 teaspoon grated ginger
- 1/4 cup water (or more as needed to thin)
- Salt and pepper to taste

For the Salad:

- 4 cups mixed salad greens (such as lettuce, spinach, or arugula)
- 1 cucumber, thinly sliced
- 1 red bell pepper, thinly sliced
- 1 carrot, shredded
- 1/4 cup chopped fresh cilantro
- 1/4 cup chopped fresh mint

- 1/4 cup chopped roasted peanuts
- Lime wedges for serving

Instructions:

For the Grilled Beef:

1. In a bowl, whisk together the soy sauce, fish sauce, minced garlic, brown sugar, grated ginger, ground coriander, chili flakes (if using), salt, and pepper to make the marinade.
2. Place the flank steak or sirloin steak in a shallow dish and pour the marinade over the steak, turning to coat evenly. Let it marinate for at least 30 minutes, or overnight in the refrigerator for deeper flavor.
3. Preheat your grill to medium-high heat. Remove the steak from the marinade and discard any excess marinade.
4. Grill the steak for about 4-6 minutes per side, or until it reaches your desired level of doneness. Transfer the grilled steak to a cutting board and let it rest for a few minutes before slicing thinly against the grain.

For the Peanut Dressing:

1. In a small bowl, whisk together the peanut butter, soy sauce, rice vinegar, honey, sesame oil, minced garlic, grated ginger, water, salt, and pepper until smooth. If the dressing is too thick, add more water, a tablespoon at a time, until you reach your desired consistency.

Assembly:

1. In a large bowl, combine the mixed salad greens, sliced cucumber, sliced red bell pepper, shredded carrot, chopped fresh cilantro, and chopped fresh mint.
2. Add the sliced grilled beef to the salad.
3. Drizzle the peanut dressing over the salad and toss gently to coat everything evenly.
4. Sprinkle the chopped roasted peanuts over the top of the salad.
5. Serve the Grilled Thai Beef Salad with Peanut Dressing immediately, with lime wedges on the side for squeezing over the top.

6. Enjoy your vibrant and flavorful salad!

This Grilled Thai Beef Salad with Peanut Dressing is perfect for a light and refreshing meal, packed with bold flavors and crunchy textures. It's great for a summer barbecue or a quick and easy weeknight dinner.

Campfire Veggie Stir-Fry with Tofu

Ingredients:

For the Stir-Fry Sauce:

- 1/4 cup soy sauce
- 2 tablespoons hoisin sauce
- 1 tablespoon rice vinegar
- 1 tablespoon sesame oil
- 1 tablespoon brown sugar
- 2 cloves garlic, minced
- 1 teaspoon grated ginger
- 1 teaspoon cornstarch

For the Stir-Fry:

- 1 block firm tofu, drained and cubed
- 2 tablespoons soy sauce
- 2 tablespoons cornstarch
- 2 tablespoons vegetable oil
- 1 onion, thinly sliced
- 2 bell peppers, thinly sliced
- 1 zucchini, thinly sliced
- 1 cup sliced mushrooms
- 2 cups broccoli florets
- Cooked rice or noodles, for serving
- Sesame seeds and sliced green onions, for garnish (optional)

Instructions:

1. Prepare the Stir-Fry Sauce:

In a small bowl, whisk together the soy sauce, hoisin sauce, rice vinegar, sesame oil, brown sugar, minced garlic, grated ginger, and cornstarch until well combined. Set aside.

2. Prepare the Tofu:

- Place the cubed tofu in a bowl and toss with 2 tablespoons of soy sauce.
- Sprinkle the cornstarch over the tofu and toss until evenly coated.

3. Cook the Tofu:

- Heat 1 tablespoon of vegetable oil in a large skillet or wok over the campfire.
- Add the tofu cubes to the skillet and cook until golden and crispy on all sides, about 5-7 minutes. Remove from the skillet and set aside.

4. Cook the Vegetables:

- In the same skillet, add another tablespoon of vegetable oil.
- Add the sliced onion, bell peppers, zucchini, mushrooms, and broccoli florets to the skillet. Cook, stirring frequently, until the vegetables are tender-crisp, about 5-7 minutes.

5. Combine:

- Return the cooked tofu to the skillet with the vegetables.
- Pour the prepared stir-fry sauce over the tofu and vegetables in the skillet. Stir well to coat everything evenly.

6. Serve:

- Serve the campfire veggie stir-fry with tofu over cooked rice or noodles.
- Garnish with sesame seeds and sliced green onions, if desired.

7. Enjoy!

This campfire veggie stir-fry with tofu is packed with flavor and nutrients, making it a satisfying and healthy outdoor meal option. Adjust the vegetables according to your preferences, and feel free to add any additional ingredients you like, such as baby corn, snap peas, or water chestnuts.

Foil Packet Lemon Dill Salmon with Green Beans

Ingredients:

- 4 salmon fillets
- 2 cups fresh green beans, trimmed
- 2 tablespoons olive oil
- 2 tablespoons fresh lemon juice
- 2 cloves garlic, minced
- 2 tablespoons chopped fresh dill
- Salt and pepper to taste
- Lemon slices for garnish
- Fresh dill sprigs for garnish

Instructions:

1. Preheat your grill to medium-high heat.
2. Tear off four large pieces of aluminum foil, each about 12x18 inches in size.
3. In a small bowl, whisk together the olive oil, lemon juice, minced garlic, chopped fresh dill, salt, and pepper to make the marinade.
4. Place one salmon fillet in the center of each piece of foil.
5. Divide the trimmed green beans evenly among the foil packets, arranging them around the salmon fillets.
6. Drizzle the marinade over the salmon fillets and green beans in each foil packet.
7. Fold the sides of each foil packet over the salmon and green beans to cover them completely, then fold up the ends to seal, creating a tight packet.
8. Place the foil packets on the preheated grill and cook for about 10-12 minutes, or until the salmon is cooked through and flakes easily with a fork, and the green beans are tender-crisp.
9. Carefully open the foil packets, being cautious of the steam.
10. Transfer the salmon fillets and green beans to serving plates or a platter.
11. Garnish with lemon slices and fresh dill sprigs before serving.
12. Serve hot and enjoy your delicious and flavorful foil packet lemon dill salmon with green beans straight from the grill!

This foil packet lemon dill salmon with green beans is not only easy to make but also results in tender and flavorful salmon with perfectly cooked green beans. It's perfect for a quick and satisfying outdoor meal.

Grilled Moroccan Lamb Kebabs with Yogurt Sauce

Ingredients:

For the Lamb Kebabs:

- 1.5 lbs lamb leg or shoulder, trimmed and cut into 1-inch cubes
- 2 tablespoons olive oil
- 2 cloves garlic, minced
- 2 teaspoons ground cumin
- 2 teaspoons ground coriander
- 1 teaspoon smoked paprika
- 1/2 teaspoon ground cinnamon
- 1/2 teaspoon ground ginger
- 1/2 teaspoon ground turmeric
- 1/4 teaspoon cayenne pepper (optional)
- Salt and pepper to taste
- Wooden or metal skewers

For the Yogurt Sauce:

- 1 cup Greek yogurt
- 1 tablespoon lemon juice
- 1 tablespoon chopped fresh mint
- 1 tablespoon chopped fresh cilantro
- 1 clove garlic, minced
- Salt and pepper to taste

For Serving:

- Warm pita bread or flatbread
- Sliced tomatoes
- Sliced cucumbers
- Sliced red onion
- Fresh lemon wedges

Instructions:

For the Lamb Kebabs:

1. In a bowl, combine the olive oil, minced garlic, ground cumin, ground coriander, smoked paprika, ground cinnamon, ground ginger, ground turmeric, cayenne pepper (if using), salt, and pepper. Mix well to make a marinade.
2. Add the cubed lamb to the marinade, tossing until the lamb is evenly coated. Cover the bowl and let the lamb marinate in the refrigerator for at least 1 hour, or overnight for best flavor.
3. If using wooden skewers, soak them in water for at least 30 minutes to prevent them from burning on the grill.
4. Preheat your grill to medium-high heat.
5. Thread the marinated lamb cubes onto the skewers, dividing them evenly among the skewers.
6. Grill the lamb kebabs for about 8-10 minutes, turning occasionally, until the lamb is cooked to your desired level of doneness and has nice grill marks.

For the Yogurt Sauce:

1. In a small bowl, combine the Greek yogurt, lemon juice, chopped fresh mint, chopped fresh cilantro, minced garlic, salt, and pepper. Mix well to combine.
2. Taste the yogurt sauce and adjust the seasoning with more salt and pepper if needed.

Assembly:

1. Serve the grilled Moroccan lamb kebabs hot, with warm pita bread or flatbread, sliced tomatoes, sliced cucumbers, sliced red onion, fresh lemon wedges, and the yogurt sauce on the side for dipping.
2. Enjoy your flavorful and aromatic grilled Moroccan lamb kebabs with yogurt sauce!

These grilled Moroccan lamb kebabs are packed with spices and flavors that will transport you to North Africa with every bite. They're perfect for a summer barbecue or outdoor gathering, and the yogurt sauce adds a cool and refreshing contrast to the savory lamb.

Campfire Ratatouille Stuffed Peppers

Ingredients:

- 4 large bell peppers (any color), halved and seeds removed
- 2 tablespoons olive oil
- 1 onion, diced
- 2 cloves garlic, minced
- 1 small eggplant, diced
- 1 zucchini, diced
- 1 yellow squash, diced
- 1 red bell pepper, diced
- 1 yellow bell pepper, diced
- 1 can (14 oz) diced tomatoes, drained
- 2 tablespoons tomato paste
- 1 teaspoon dried thyme
- 1 teaspoon dried oregano
- Salt and pepper to taste
- 1/4 cup grated Parmesan cheese
- Fresh basil leaves for garnish

Instructions:

1. Preheat your campfire or grill to medium heat.
2. Heat the olive oil in a large skillet over the campfire. Add the diced onion and garlic, and cook until softened and fragrant, about 2-3 minutes.
3. Add the diced eggplant, zucchini, yellow squash, diced red bell pepper, and diced yellow bell pepper to the skillet. Cook, stirring occasionally, until the vegetables are tender, about 8-10 minutes.
4. Stir in the drained diced tomatoes, tomato paste, dried thyme, and dried oregano. Season with salt and pepper to taste. Cook for an additional 5 minutes, allowing the flavors to meld together.
5. While the ratatouille mixture is cooking, prepare the bell peppers. Slice each bell pepper in half lengthwise and remove the seeds and membranes.
6. Once the ratatouille mixture is ready, spoon it into each halved bell pepper, filling them to the top.
7. Sprinkle the grated Parmesan cheese evenly over the stuffed peppers.
8. Wrap each stuffed pepper individually in aluminum foil, creating a tight packet.

9. Place the foil-wrapped stuffed peppers on the preheated campfire or grill. Cook for about 20-25 minutes, or until the peppers are tender and the filling is heated through.
10. Carefully remove the foil packets from the campfire or grill and let them cool for a few minutes.
11. Unwrap the foil packets and garnish the stuffed peppers with fresh basil leaves before serving.
12. Serve the Campfire Ratatouille Stuffed Peppers hot as a main course or as a side dish alongside grilled meats or seafood.

Enjoy the delightful combination of flavors and the rustic charm of these Campfire Ratatouille Stuffed Peppers, perfect for outdoor dining or camping adventures!

Grilled Octopus with Chimichurri Sauce

Ingredients:

For the Grilled Octopus:

- 2-3 lbs octopus, cleaned and tentacles separated
- 1/4 cup olive oil
- 2 cloves garlic, minced
- Juice of 1 lemon
- Salt and pepper to taste

For the Chimichurri Sauce:

- 1 cup fresh parsley leaves, finely chopped
- 1/4 cup fresh cilantro leaves, finely chopped
- 3 cloves garlic, minced
- 2 tablespoons red wine vinegar
- 1/2 teaspoon red pepper flakes (adjust to taste)
- 1/2 cup extra virgin olive oil
- Salt and pepper to taste

Instructions:

1. Prepare the Grilled Octopus:

   1. In a large pot, bring water to a boil. Add the octopus tentacles and cook for about 30-45 minutes, or until tender. You can also add aromatics such as bay leaves, peppercorns, or onion to the boiling water for added flavor.
   2. Once the octopus is tender, remove it from the pot and let it cool slightly.
   3. In a bowl, mix together the olive oil, minced garlic, lemon juice, salt, and pepper. Brush this mixture over the cooked octopus tentacles.
   4. Preheat your grill to medium-high heat. Grill the octopus tentacles for about 2-3 minutes per side, or until charred and slightly crispy.

2. Prepare the Chimichurri Sauce:

1. In a bowl, combine the finely chopped parsley, cilantro, minced garlic, red wine vinegar, red pepper flakes, extra virgin olive oil, salt, and pepper. Mix well to combine.
2. Taste the chimichurri sauce and adjust the seasoning according to your preference. You can add more vinegar for acidity or more red pepper flakes for heat.

3. Serve:

1. Arrange the grilled octopus tentacles on a serving platter.
2. Drizzle the chimichurri sauce over the grilled octopus or serve it on the side as a dipping sauce.
3. Garnish with additional fresh herbs, lemon wedges, or a drizzle of olive oil if desired.
4. Serve the grilled octopus with chimichurri sauce immediately while still warm.

Enjoy the tender and flavorful grilled octopus with the vibrant and herbaceous chimichurri sauce for a delicious and memorable dining experience!

Foil Packet BBQ Chicken and Potatoes

Ingredients:

- 4 boneless, skinless chicken breasts
- 4 medium potatoes, thinly sliced
- 1 cup barbecue sauce
- 1/2 cup shredded cheddar cheese (optional)
- Salt and pepper to taste
- Chopped fresh parsley or green onions for garnish (optional)

Instructions:

1. Preheat your grill to medium-high heat.
2. Tear off four large pieces of aluminum foil, each about 12x18 inches in size.
3. Season each chicken breast with salt and pepper to taste.
4. Place one seasoned chicken breast in the center of each piece of foil.
5. Arrange the thinly sliced potatoes around each chicken breast.
6. Spoon about 1/4 cup of barbecue sauce over each chicken breast, spreading it evenly.
7. If using, sprinkle shredded cheddar cheese over the chicken and potatoes.
8. Fold the sides of each foil packet over the chicken and potatoes to cover them completely, then fold up the ends to seal, creating a tight packet.
9. Place the foil packets on the preheated grill and cook for about 20-25 minutes, or until the chicken is cooked through and the potatoes are tender.
10. Carefully open the foil packets, being cautious of the steam.
11. Transfer the chicken and potatoes to serving plates or a platter.
12. Garnish with chopped fresh parsley or green onions, if desired.
13. Serve hot and enjoy your delicious and easy foil packet BBQ chicken and potatoes straight from the grill!

This foil packet BBQ chicken and potatoes is perfect for a quick and satisfying outdoor meal. It's packed with flavor and requires minimal cleanup, making it a great option for camping trips or backyard cookouts.

Campfire Eggplant Involtini with Ricotta and Marinara

Ingredients:

For the Eggplant:

- 2 medium eggplants, thinly sliced lengthwise
- Olive oil for brushing
- Salt and pepper to taste

For the Ricotta Filling:

- 1 cup ricotta cheese
- 1/4 cup grated Parmesan cheese
- 1 egg
- 2 tablespoons chopped fresh basil
- 1 clove garlic, minced
- Salt and pepper to taste

For the Marinara Sauce:

- 2 cups marinara sauce (store-bought or homemade)
- 1/4 cup chopped fresh basil
- 1/4 cup grated Parmesan cheese

For Serving:

- Fresh basil leaves for garnish

Instructions:

1. Preheat the Grill:

   1. Preheat your grill to medium-high heat.

2. Prepare the Eggplant:

1. Thinly slice the eggplants lengthwise, about 1/4 inch thick.
2. Brush both sides of the eggplant slices with olive oil and season with salt and pepper.

3. Grill the Eggplant:

    1. Place the eggplant slices on the preheated grill and cook for about 2-3 minutes per side, or until tender and lightly charred. Remove from the grill and set aside.

4. Prepare the Ricotta Filling:

    1. In a bowl, combine the ricotta cheese, grated Parmesan cheese, egg, chopped fresh basil, minced garlic, salt, and pepper. Mix well to combine.

5. Assemble the Involtini:

    1. Place a spoonful of the ricotta filling onto one end of each grilled eggplant slice.
    2. Roll up the eggplant slices to enclose the filling, forming small bundles.

6. Prepare the Marinara Sauce:

    1. In a small saucepan or heatproof dish, heat the marinara sauce over the campfire or grill until warmed through.
    2. Stir in the chopped fresh basil and grated Parmesan cheese.

7. Cook the Involtini:

    1. Place the rolled eggplant involtini seam-side down in a heatproof dish or foil tray.
    2. Pour the warm marinara sauce over the eggplant involtini.

8. Grill the Involtini:

    1. Place the dish or foil tray with the eggplant involtini on the grill over indirect heat.
    2. Close the grill lid and cook for about 10-15 minutes, or until the cheese is melted and bubbly.

9. Serve:

    1. Remove the eggplant involtini from the grill and garnish with fresh basil leaves.
    2. Serve hot and enjoy your delicious Campfire Eggplant Involtini with Ricotta and Marinara!

This dish is perfect for a cozy outdoor meal with friends and family. The grilled eggplant adds a smoky flavor, while the creamy ricotta filling and marinara sauce create a comforting and satisfying dish. Enjoy it as a main course or as a side dish alongside your favorite grilled meats or seafood.

Grilled Shrimp and Pineapple Skewers with Coconut Rice

Ingredients:

For the Shrimp and Pineapple Skewers:

- 1 lb large shrimp, peeled and deveined
- 1 large pineapple, peeled, cored, and cut into chunks
- 2 tablespoons olive oil
- 2 cloves garlic, minced
- 1 teaspoon paprika
- 1/2 teaspoon chili powder
- Salt and pepper to taste
- Wooden or metal skewers

For the Coconut Rice:

- 1 cup jasmine rice
- 1 cup coconut milk
- 1 cup water
- 1/2 teaspoon salt
- 1 tablespoon chopped fresh cilantro (optional)

Instructions:

1. Prepare the Shrimp and Pineapple Skewers:

    1. If using wooden skewers, soak them in water for about 30 minutes to prevent burning.
    2. In a bowl, combine the olive oil, minced garlic, paprika, chili powder, salt, and pepper. Mix well.
    3. Thread the shrimp and pineapple chunks alternately onto the skewers.
    4. Brush the skewers with the olive oil mixture, coating them evenly.

2. Grill the Skewers:

1. Preheat your grill to medium-high heat.
2. Place the skewers on the grill and cook for about 2-3 minutes per side, or until the shrimp are pink and opaque and the pineapple is lightly charred.
3. Remove the skewers from the grill and set aside.

3. Prepare the Coconut Rice:

1. In a saucepan, combine the jasmine rice, coconut milk, water, and salt.
2. Bring the mixture to a boil over medium-high heat.
3. Once boiling, reduce the heat to low, cover, and simmer for about 15-20 minutes, or until the rice is cooked and the liquid is absorbed.
4. Fluff the rice with a fork and stir in the chopped fresh cilantro, if using.

4. Serve:

1. Serve the grilled shrimp and pineapple skewers alongside the coconut rice.
2. Garnish with additional chopped cilantro, if desired.
3. Enjoy your delicious Grilled Shrimp and Pineapple Skewers with Coconut Rice!

This dish is bursting with tropical flavors and is sure to be a hit at your next outdoor gathering. The juicy shrimp, sweet pineapple, and creamy coconut rice come together for a delightful combination that will transport you to a sunny beach paradise.

Campfire BBQ Brisket with Homemade BBQ Sauce

Ingredients:

For the Brisket:

- 1 whole beef brisket (about 4-5 pounds)
- 2 tablespoons brown sugar
- 2 tablespoons paprika
- 1 tablespoon garlic powder
- 1 tablespoon onion powder
- 1 tablespoon chili powder
- 1 tablespoon ground cumin
- 1 tablespoon ground black pepper
- 1 tablespoon kosher salt
- Olive oil for rubbing

For the Homemade BBQ Sauce:

- 1 cup ketchup
- 1/4 cup apple cider vinegar
- 1/4 cup brown sugar
- 2 tablespoons Worcestershire sauce
- 1 tablespoon Dijon mustard
- 1 tablespoon paprika
- 1 teaspoon garlic powder
- Salt and pepper to taste

Instructions:

1. Prepare the Brisket:

   1. In a small bowl, combine the brown sugar, paprika, garlic powder, onion powder, chili powder, ground cumin, black pepper, and kosher salt to make the dry rub.
   2. Pat the brisket dry with paper towels and trim any excess fat.

3. Rub the brisket all over with olive oil, then coat it evenly with the dry rub mixture, pressing it into the meat.
4. Wrap the brisket tightly in plastic wrap and refrigerate for at least 4 hours, or overnight, to allow the flavors to penetrate the meat.

2. Cook the Brisket:

1. Preheat your campfire or smoker to 225°F (110°C).
2. Place the brisket directly on the grill grate or in a smoker, fat-side up.
3. Close the lid and cook the brisket low and slow for about 1 hour per pound, or until the internal temperature reaches 195-205°F (90-96°C).
4. During the cooking process, periodically check the temperature and spritz the brisket with water or apple cider vinegar to keep it moist.

3. Make the Homemade BBQ Sauce:

1. In a saucepan, combine the ketchup, apple cider vinegar, brown sugar, Worcestershire sauce, Dijon mustard, paprika, garlic powder, salt, and pepper.
2. Bring the mixture to a simmer over medium heat, stirring occasionally.
3. Reduce the heat to low and let the sauce simmer for about 15-20 minutes, or until it has thickened to your desired consistency.
4. Taste and adjust the seasoning as needed.

4. Serve:

1. Once the brisket reaches the desired temperature, remove it from the grill and let it rest for about 15-20 minutes before slicing.
2. Slice the brisket against the grain into thin slices.
3. Serve the sliced brisket with the homemade BBQ sauce on the side.
4. Enjoy your delicious Campfire BBQ Brisket with Homemade BBQ Sauce!

This slow-cooked brisket is tender, juicy, and packed with flavor, and the homemade BBQ sauce adds the perfect tangy sweetness to complement the rich meat. It's sure to be a hit at your next outdoor gathering or barbecue!

Foil Packet Mediterranean Salmon with Olives and Tomatoes

Ingredients:

- 4 salmon fillets
- 1 cup cherry tomatoes, halved
- 1/2 cup pitted Kalamata olives, halved
- 2 tablespoons capers
- 2 cloves garlic, minced
- 2 tablespoons chopped fresh parsley
- 2 tablespoons olive oil
- 1 tablespoon lemon juice
- Salt and pepper to taste
- Lemon slices for garnish
- Fresh parsley for garnish

Instructions:

1. Preheat your grill to medium-high heat.
2. Tear off four large pieces of aluminum foil, each about 12x18 inches in size.
3. Place a salmon fillet in the center of each piece of foil.
4. In a bowl, combine the cherry tomatoes, Kalamata olives, capers, minced garlic, chopped fresh parsley, olive oil, lemon juice, salt, and pepper. Mix well to combine.
5. Spoon the tomato and olive mixture over each salmon fillet, dividing it evenly.
6. Fold the sides of each foil packet over the salmon and tomato mixture to cover them completely, then fold up the ends to seal, creating a tight packet.
7. Place the foil packets on the preheated grill and cook for about 10-12 minutes, or until the salmon is cooked through and flakes easily with a fork.
8. Carefully open the foil packets, being cautious of the steam.
9. Transfer the salmon fillets and tomato mixture to serving plates or a platter.
10. Garnish with lemon slices and fresh parsley before serving.
11. Serve hot and enjoy your delicious Foil Packet Mediterranean Salmon with Olives and Tomatoes!

This dish is bursting with Mediterranean flavors and is perfect for a quick and easy outdoor meal. The salmon stays moist and flavorful thanks to the foil packet cooking method, and the combination of olives, tomatoes, and capers adds a delicious burst of flavor. Enjoy it with a side of rice or a fresh green salad for a complete and satisfying meal.

Grilled Chicken Shawarma Wraps with Tahini Sauce

Ingredients:

For the Chicken Shawarma:

- 1 lb boneless, skinless chicken thighs
- 2 cloves garlic, minced
- 2 tablespoons lemon juice
- 2 tablespoons olive oil
- 1 teaspoon ground cumin
- 1 teaspoon ground paprika
- 1/2 teaspoon ground turmeric
- 1/2 teaspoon ground coriander
- 1/4 teaspoon ground cinnamon
- Salt and pepper to taste

For the Tahini Sauce:

- 1/4 cup tahini paste
- 2 tablespoons lemon juice
- 2 tablespoons water
- 1 clove garlic, minced
- Salt to taste

For Serving:

- Pita bread or wraps
- Sliced tomatoes
- Sliced cucumbers
- Sliced red onions
- Chopped fresh parsley or cilantro

Instructions:

1. Marinate the Chicken:

1. In a bowl, combine the minced garlic, lemon juice, olive oil, ground cumin, ground paprika, ground turmeric, ground coriander, ground cinnamon, salt, and pepper.
2. Add the chicken thighs to the marinade, making sure they are well coated. Cover and refrigerate for at least 1 hour, or overnight for best flavor.

2. Make the Tahini Sauce:

1. In a small bowl, whisk together the tahini paste, lemon juice, water, minced garlic, and salt until smooth and creamy. If the sauce is too thick, you can add more water, a tablespoon at a time, until you reach your desired consistency.

3. Grill the Chicken:

1. Preheat your grill to medium-high heat.
2. Remove the chicken thighs from the marinade and discard any excess marinade.
3. Grill the chicken thighs for about 6-8 minutes per side, or until they are cooked through and have nice grill marks. The internal temperature should reach 165°F (74°C).
4. Once cooked, transfer the chicken thighs to a cutting board and let them rest for a few minutes before slicing them into thin strips.

4. Assemble the Wraps:

1. Warm the pita bread or wraps on the grill for a few seconds on each side.
2. Spread a generous amount of tahini sauce on each piece of pita bread or wrap.
3. Arrange some sliced chicken shawarma on top of the tahini sauce.
4. Add sliced tomatoes, cucumbers, and red onions on top of the chicken.
5. Sprinkle with chopped fresh parsley or cilantro.
6. Roll up the wraps tightly and secure them with toothpicks if needed.

5. Serve:

1. Serve the Grilled Chicken Shawarma Wraps with extra tahini sauce on the side for dipping.
2. Enjoy your delicious and flavorful wraps!

These Grilled Chicken Shawarma Wraps with Tahini Sauce are packed with Middle Eastern flavors and make for a satisfying and nutritious meal. They're perfect for a casual outdoor lunch or dinner with friends and family.

Campfire Stuffed Acorn Squash with Quinoa and Cranberries

Ingredients:

- 2 acorn squash, halved and seeds removed
- 1 cup quinoa, rinsed
- 2 cups vegetable broth or water
- 1/2 cup dried cranberries
- 1/2 cup chopped pecans or walnuts
- 1/4 cup chopped fresh parsley
- 2 tablespoons olive oil
- 2 cloves garlic, minced
- 1 teaspoon ground cumin
- 1 teaspoon ground cinnamon
- Salt and pepper to taste

Instructions:

1. Prepare the Acorn Squash:

   1. Preheat your campfire or grill to medium heat.
   2. Cut the acorn squash in half lengthwise and scoop out the seeds and stringy pulp with a spoon.
   3. Place the acorn squash halves, cut side up, on a large piece of heavy-duty aluminum foil.

2. Cook the Quinoa:

   1. In a saucepan, combine the quinoa and vegetable broth or water.
   2. Bring the mixture to a boil over medium-high heat.
   3. Reduce the heat to low, cover, and simmer for about 15-20 minutes, or until the quinoa is cooked and the liquid is absorbed.
   4. Fluff the quinoa with a fork and remove it from the heat.

3. Prepare the Filling:

1. In a large bowl, combine the cooked quinoa, dried cranberries, chopped pecans or walnuts, chopped fresh parsley, olive oil, minced garlic, ground cumin, ground cinnamon, salt, and pepper. Mix well to combine.

4. Stuff the Acorn Squash:

   1. Divide the quinoa filling evenly among the acorn squash halves, filling the cavities.
   2. Fold the edges of the aluminum foil over the stuffed squash to create a sealed packet.

5. Cook the Stuffed Acorn Squash:

   1. Place the foil packet containing the stuffed acorn squash on the preheated campfire or grill.
   2. Cook for about 20-25 minutes, or until the squash is tender and the filling is heated through.

6. Serve:

   1. Carefully open the foil packet and transfer the stuffed acorn squash to serving plates or a platter.
   2. Serve hot and enjoy your delicious Campfire Stuffed Acorn Squash with Quinoa and Cranberries!

This dish is perfect for a cozy outdoor meal and is packed with flavor and nutrition. The combination of sweet acorn squash, nutty quinoa, tart cranberries, and aromatic spices is sure to be a hit with everyone around the campfire.

Grilled Scallops with Citrus-Herb Butter

Ingredients:

For the Citrus-Herb Butter:

- 1/2 cup unsalted butter, softened
- Zest of 1 lemon
- Zest of 1 lime
- 2 tablespoons chopped fresh parsley
- 1 tablespoon chopped fresh chives
- 1 tablespoon chopped fresh thyme
- Salt and pepper to taste

For the Scallops:

- 1 lb fresh scallops, cleaned
- Olive oil for brushing
- Salt and pepper to taste
- Lemon wedges for serving

Instructions:

1. Prepare the Citrus-Herb Butter:

   1. In a small bowl, combine the softened butter, lemon zest, lime zest, chopped fresh parsley, chopped fresh chives, chopped fresh thyme, salt, and pepper. Mix well to combine.
   2. Transfer the citrus-herb butter mixture to a piece of plastic wrap and shape it into a log. Wrap tightly and refrigerate until firm.

2. Prepare the Scallops:

   1. Preheat your grill to medium-high heat.
   2. Pat the scallops dry with paper towels to remove excess moisture.

3. Thread the scallops onto skewers, if desired, to make them easier to handle on the grill.
4. Brush both sides of the scallops with olive oil and season with salt and pepper.

3. Grill the Scallops:

1. Place the scallops directly on the preheated grill grates.
2. Grill the scallops for about 2-3 minutes per side, or until they are opaque and have grill marks.
3. Be careful not to overcook the scallops, as they can become tough and rubbery.

4. Serve:

1. Remove the scallops from the grill and transfer them to a serving platter.
2. Slice a few rounds of the citrus-herb butter and place them on top of the hot grilled scallops, allowing the butter to melt and coat the scallops.
3. Serve immediately with lemon wedges on the side for squeezing over the scallops.

5. Enjoy:

1. Enjoy your delicious Grilled Scallops with Citrus-Herb Butter as a main course or appetizer!

This dish is sure to impress with its combination of succulent scallops and flavorful citrus-herb butter. It's perfect for a special outdoor meal or as part of a seafood feast.

Foil Packet Garlic Herb Steak and Potatoes

Ingredients:

- 1 lb sirloin steak, cut into bite-sized pieces
- 4 medium potatoes, diced into small cubes
- 1 onion, diced
- 2 cloves garlic, minced
- 2 tablespoons olive oil
- 2 tablespoons Worcestershire sauce
- 1 tablespoon soy sauce
- 1 teaspoon dried thyme
- 1 teaspoon dried rosemary
- Salt and pepper to taste
- Fresh parsley for garnish

Instructions:

1. Prepare the Foil Packets:

   1. Preheat your grill to medium-high heat.
   2. Tear off four large pieces of aluminum foil, each about 12x18 inches in size.
   3. In a large bowl, combine the diced steak, diced potatoes, diced onion, minced garlic, olive oil, Worcestershire sauce, soy sauce, dried thyme, dried rosemary, salt, and pepper. Mix well to coat everything evenly.
   4. Divide the steak and potato mixture evenly among the four pieces of foil, placing it in the center of each foil piece.

2. Seal the Foil Packets:

   1. Fold the sides of each foil packet over the steak and potato mixture to cover them completely, then fold up the ends to seal, creating a tight packet.
   2. Make sure the packets are well-sealed to prevent any juices from leaking out during cooking.

3. Grill the Foil Packets:

1. Place the foil packets directly on the preheated grill grates.
2. Grill the packets for about 10-12 minutes per side, or until the steak is cooked to your desired level of doneness and the potatoes are tender.
3. Carefully open the foil packets, being cautious of the steam.

4. Serve:

1. Transfer the contents of each foil packet to serving plates or bowls.
2. Garnish with fresh parsley, if desired.
3. Serve hot and enjoy your delicious Foil Packet Garlic Herb Steak and Potatoes!

This dish is easy to prepare, cooks quickly, and requires minimal cleanup, making it perfect for outdoor dining or camping trips. The steak and potatoes are infused with garlic and herb flavors, creating a comforting and satisfying meal that's sure to be a hit with family and friends.

Campfire Ratatouille Flatbread Pizza

Ingredients:

For the Ratatouille:

- 1 small eggplant, diced
- 1 small zucchini, diced
- 1 small yellow squash, diced
- 1 bell pepper, diced
- 1 onion, diced
- 2 cloves garlic, minced
- 2 tablespoons olive oil
- 1 can (14 oz) diced tomatoes
- 1 teaspoon dried oregano
- 1 teaspoon dried basil
- Salt and pepper to taste

For the Flatbread Pizza:

- 4 pieces of flatbread or naan
- 1 cup shredded mozzarella cheese
- Fresh basil leaves, torn
- Red pepper flakes (optional)

Instructions:

1. Prepare the Ratatouille:

   1. Heat the olive oil in a large skillet or cast-iron pan over medium heat.
   2. Add the diced eggplant, zucchini, yellow squash, bell pepper, onion, and minced garlic to the pan.
   3. Cook, stirring occasionally, for about 8-10 minutes, or until the vegetables are softened and starting to brown.
   4. Stir in the diced tomatoes, dried oregano, dried basil, salt, and pepper.

5. Continue cooking for another 5-7 minutes, or until the flavors are well combined and the ratatouille has thickened slightly. Remove from heat and set aside.

2. Assemble the Flatbread Pizzas:

   1. Preheat your campfire or grill to medium heat.
   2. Place the flatbread or naan pieces on a clean surface.
   3. Spread a layer of the ratatouille mixture evenly over each flatbread.
   4. Sprinkle shredded mozzarella cheese over the ratatouille layer.
   5. Place the assembled flatbread pizzas on a grill-safe pan or directly on the grill grates.

3. Cook the Flatbread Pizzas:

   1. Close the lid of the grill and cook the pizzas for about 5-7 minutes, or until the cheese is melted and bubbly, and the flatbread is crisp.
   2. Keep an eye on the pizzas to prevent burning, rotating them if necessary for even cooking.

4. Serve:

   1. Remove the flatbread pizzas from the grill and transfer them to a cutting board.
   2. Sprinkle torn fresh basil leaves and red pepper flakes (if using) over the pizzas.
   3. Slice the pizzas into wedges or squares and serve hot.

5. Enjoy:

   1. Enjoy your delicious Campfire Ratatouille Flatbread Pizzas with friends and family around the campfire!

These pizzas are loaded with colorful and flavorful ratatouille vegetables, gooey melted cheese, and aromatic herbs, making them a satisfying and wholesome outdoor meal.

Feel free to customize the toppings or add additional cheese or herbs to suit your taste preferences.

Grilled Tuna Nicoise Salad with Dijon Vinaigrette

Ingredients:

For the Salad:

- 2 tuna steaks (about 6 oz each)
- 6 cups mixed salad greens (such as arugula, spinach, and lettuce)
- 1 cup cherry tomatoes, halved
- 1 cup cooked green beans, trimmed
- 1/2 cup sliced black olives
- 4 hard-boiled eggs, sliced
- 4 small red potatoes, boiled and quartered
- 2 tablespoons capers (optional)
- Salt and pepper to taste

For the Dijon Vinaigrette:

- 1/4 cup extra-virgin olive oil
- 2 tablespoons red wine vinegar
- 1 tablespoon Dijon mustard
- 1 teaspoon honey or maple syrup
- 1 clove garlic, minced
- Salt and pepper to taste

For Garnish:

- Fresh parsley, chopped
- Lemon wedges

Instructions:

1. Prepare the Tuna:

   1. Preheat your grill to medium-high heat.
   2. Season the tuna steaks with salt and pepper on both sides.

3. Grill the tuna steaks for about 2-3 minutes per side, or until desired doneness (for medium-rare, the internal temperature should reach 125°F or 52°C).
4. Remove the tuna steaks from the grill and let them rest for a few minutes before slicing.

2. Prepare the Salad:

   1. In a large serving bowl, arrange the mixed salad greens.
   2. Top the greens with cherry tomatoes, cooked green beans, sliced black olives, hard-boiled eggs, and quartered red potatoes.
   3. Scatter capers over the salad, if using.

3. Make the Dijon Vinaigrette:

   1. In a small bowl, whisk together the extra-virgin olive oil, red wine vinegar, Dijon mustard, honey or maple syrup, minced garlic, salt, and pepper until well combined.

4. Assemble the Salad:

   1. Drizzle the Dijon vinaigrette over the salad.
   2. Gently toss the salad to coat the ingredients evenly with the dressing.
   3. Arrange the sliced grilled tuna on top of the salad.

5. Garnish and Serve:

   1. Garnish the salad with chopped fresh parsley and lemon wedges.
   2. Serve the Grilled Tuna Nicoise Salad immediately, and enjoy!

This salad is a delicious and satisfying meal that's perfect for a light lunch or dinner outdoors. The combination of fresh greens, grilled tuna, and flavorful Dijon vinaigrette creates a vibrant and healthy dish that's sure to impress.

Campfire Stuffed Portobello Mushrooms with Sun-Dried Tomatoes and Feta

Ingredients:

- 4 large portobello mushrooms, stems removed
- 1/2 cup sun-dried tomatoes, chopped
- 1/2 cup crumbled feta cheese
- 2 cloves garlic, minced
- 2 tablespoons chopped fresh parsley
- 2 tablespoons olive oil
- Salt and pepper to taste

Instructions:

1. Prepare the Portobello Mushrooms:

   1. Preheat your campfire or grill to medium heat.
   2. Clean the portobello mushrooms by wiping them with a damp paper towel to remove any dirt.
   3. Remove the stems from the mushrooms and discard them.

2. Prepare the Filling:

   1. In a bowl, combine the chopped sun-dried tomatoes, crumbled feta cheese, minced garlic, chopped fresh parsley, and olive oil. Mix well to combine.
   2. Season the filling mixture with salt and pepper to taste.

3. Stuff the Portobello Mushrooms:

   1. Spoon the filling mixture into the cavity of each portobello mushroom, pressing down gently to pack the filling.
   2. Make sure to distribute the filling evenly among the mushrooms.

4. Grill the Stuffed Portobello Mushrooms:

1. Place the stuffed portobello mushrooms on the preheated grill grates.
2. Close the lid of the grill and cook the mushrooms for about 10-15 minutes, or until the mushrooms are tender and the filling is heated through.
3. Be sure to monitor the mushrooms closely to prevent burning.

5. Serve:

1. Once the stuffed portobello mushrooms are cooked, remove them from the grill and transfer them to a serving platter.
2. Garnish with additional chopped parsley, if desired.
3. Serve hot and enjoy your delicious Campfire Stuffed Portobello Mushrooms with Sun-Dried Tomatoes and Feta!

These stuffed portobello mushrooms are bursting with flavor from the savory sun-dried tomatoes, tangy feta cheese, and aromatic garlic and parsley. They make a satisfying vegetarian main dish or a delicious side dish to accompany grilled meats or other grilled vegetables.

Grilled Lamb Chops with Mint Chimichurri Sauce

Ingredients:

For the Grilled Lamb Chops:

- 8 lamb loin chops, about 1 inch thick
- 2 tablespoons olive oil
- 4 cloves garlic, minced
- 1 teaspoon dried oregano
- 1 teaspoon dried rosemary
- Salt and pepper to taste

For the Mint Chimichurri Sauce:

- 1 cup fresh mint leaves, packed
- 1 cup fresh parsley leaves, packed
- 2 cloves garlic, minced
- 1/4 cup red wine vinegar
- 1/2 cup extra-virgin olive oil
- 1 teaspoon dried oregano
- Salt and pepper to taste
- Red pepper flakes (optional)

Instructions:

1. Marinate the Lamb Chops:

    1. In a small bowl, combine the olive oil, minced garlic, dried oregano, dried rosemary, salt, and pepper.
    2. Rub the marinade all over the lamb chops, coating them evenly.
    3. Cover and refrigerate the lamb chops for at least 30 minutes to marinate.

2. Prepare the Mint Chimichurri Sauce:

1. In a food processor or blender, combine the fresh mint leaves, fresh parsley leaves, minced garlic, red wine vinegar, extra-virgin olive oil, dried oregano, salt, pepper, and red pepper flakes (if using).
2. Pulse until the herbs are finely chopped and the ingredients are well combined, but still slightly chunky.
3. Taste and adjust the seasoning as needed. Add more salt, pepper, or red pepper flakes to taste.

3. Grill the Lamb Chops:

1. Preheat your grill to medium-high heat.
2. Remove the lamb chops from the refrigerator and let them come to room temperature while the grill is heating.
3. Place the lamb chops on the preheated grill grates and cook for about 3-4 minutes per side for medium-rare, or longer to your desired level of doneness.
4. Remove the lamb chops from the grill and let them rest for a few minutes before serving.

4. Serve:

1. Arrange the grilled lamb chops on a serving platter.
2. Drizzle the mint chimichurri sauce over the lamb chops or serve it on the side.
3. Garnish with additional fresh mint leaves and parsley, if desired.
4. Serve hot and enjoy your delicious Grilled Lamb Chops with Mint Chimichurri Sauce!

These grilled lamb chops are tender, juicy, and packed with flavor from the aromatic marinade and fresh mint chimichurri sauce. They're perfect for a special outdoor meal or a backyard barbecue with friends and family.

Foil Packet Lemon Garlic Shrimp and Asparagus

Ingredients:

- 1 lb large shrimp, peeled and deveined
- 1 bunch asparagus, trimmed and cut into bite-sized pieces
- 4 cloves garlic, minced
- Zest of 1 lemon
- Juice of 1 lemon
- 2 tablespoons olive oil
- Salt and pepper, to taste
- Red pepper flakes (optional)
- Fresh parsley, chopped, for garnish

Instructions:

1. Preheat your grill to medium-high heat.
2. Cut four large pieces of heavy-duty aluminum foil, about 12x18 inches each.
3. In a bowl, combine the shrimp, asparagus, minced garlic, lemon zest, lemon juice, olive oil, salt, pepper, and red pepper flakes (if using). Toss until everything is well coated.
4. Divide the shrimp and asparagus mixture evenly among the foil pieces, placing it in the center.
5. Fold the sides of the foil over the shrimp and asparagus to create a packet. Fold the edges to seal tightly.
6. Place the foil packets on the preheated grill and cook for 8-10 minutes, or until the shrimp are pink and opaque, and the asparagus is tender-crisp.
7. Carefully open the foil packets, being cautious of the steam.
8. Sprinkle with fresh chopped parsley for garnish.
9. Serve hot and enjoy your delicious Foil Packet Lemon Garlic Shrimp and Asparagus!

This dish is bursting with flavor from the zesty lemon and garlic, and the asparagus adds a fresh and vibrant touch. It's a simple and satisfying meal that's perfect for a quick weeknight dinner or a relaxed outdoor gathering with friends and family.

Campfire Cornish Hens with Herb Butter

Ingredients:

- 2 Cornish hens
- Salt and pepper, to taste
- 4 tablespoons unsalted butter, softened
- 2 cloves garlic, minced
- 1 tablespoon chopped fresh parsley
- 1 tablespoon chopped fresh thyme
- 1 tablespoon chopped fresh rosemary
- Zest of 1 lemon
- Lemon slices, for garnish
- Fresh herbs, for garnish

Instructions:

1. Prepare your campfire or grill for medium-high heat.
2. Rinse the Cornish hens under cold water and pat dry with paper towels. Season the hens inside and out with salt and pepper.
3. In a small bowl, combine the softened butter, minced garlic, chopped parsley, chopped thyme, chopped rosemary, and lemon zest. Mix until well combined.
4. Gently loosen the skin of each Cornish hen and rub half of the herb butter mixture underneath the skin, spreading it evenly over the breast and thighs. Rub the remaining herb butter over the outside of the hens.
5. Place the Cornish hens on the grill grate or in a grill-safe pan, breast side up.
6. Cook the hens over indirect heat, with the lid closed, for about 45-60 minutes, or until they reach an internal temperature of 165°F (75°C) in the thickest part of the thigh.
7. During the last 10 minutes of cooking, you can baste the hens with any remaining herb butter and add lemon slices to the grill for garnish.
8. Once the hens are cooked through and golden brown, remove them from the grill and let them rest for a few minutes before serving.
9. Garnish the Cornish hens with fresh herbs and lemon slices before serving.
10. Serve hot and enjoy your delicious Campfire Cornish Hens with Herb Butter!

These Cornish hens are tender, juicy, and packed with flavor from the herb butter. They make for a stunning presentation and are sure to impress your guests at your next outdoor gathering.

Grilled Vegetable Platter with Balsamic Glaze

Ingredients:

- Assorted vegetables, such as:
    - Bell peppers (red, yellow, and/or orange), sliced into strips
    - Zucchini, sliced lengthwise
    - Yellow squash, sliced lengthwise
    - Eggplant, sliced into rounds
    - Red onion, sliced into rounds
    - Cherry tomatoes, left whole
- Olive oil
- Salt and pepper, to taste
- Balsamic glaze, for drizzling
- Fresh herbs, for garnish (optional)

Instructions:

1. Preheat your grill to medium-high heat.
2. Prepare the vegetables by slicing them into uniform pieces. Larger vegetables like bell peppers, zucchini, yellow squash, and eggplant can be sliced into strips or rounds. Cherry tomatoes can be left whole.
3. Brush the vegetables lightly with olive oil on both sides and season with salt and pepper.
4. Place the vegetables on the preheated grill. Cook the vegetables in batches, if necessary, to avoid overcrowding the grill.
5. Grill the vegetables for 3-5 minutes per side, or until they are tender and have grill marks.
6. Transfer the grilled vegetables to a serving platter.
7. Drizzle the vegetables with balsamic glaze, concentrating on the vegetables' natural sweetness.
8. Garnish with fresh herbs, if desired, for added flavor and visual appeal.
9. Serve the Grilled Vegetable Platter with Balsamic Glaze immediately, alongside your favorite grilled meats or as a standalone dish.

This dish is perfect for showcasing the natural flavors of seasonal vegetables and is sure to be a hit at any outdoor gathering. The balsamic glaze adds a touch of sweetness and acidity that complements the smoky flavors from the grill. Enjoy!

www.ingramcontent.com/pod-product-compliance
Lightning Source LLC
LaVergne TN
LVHW081558060526
838201LV00054B/1945